The Crisis of Fear

THE
CRISIS
OF
FEAR

Edward E. Thornton
and
Gerald L. Borchert

BROADMAN PRESS
Nashville, Tennessee

4254-40
ISBN: 0-8054-5440-3

Dewey Decimal Classification Number: 152.4
Subject Heading: FEAR

Library of Congress Catalog Card Number:
Printed in the United States of America

Unless otherwise indicated Scripture quotations are from the Revised Standard Version of the Bible, copyrighted 1946, 1952, © 1971, 1973. The quotations marked with an asterisk (*) are the author's translation.

Library of Congress Cataloging-in-Publication Data

Thornton, Edward E.
  The crisis of fear / Edward E. Thornton, Gerald L. Borchert.
    p.   cm.—(The Bible and personal crisis)
  ISBN 0-8054-5440-3 :
  1. Fear—Religious aspects—Christianity. 2. Consolation.
I. Borchert, Gerald L. II. Title. III. Series.
BV4908.5.T46   1988
248.8'6—dc19   88-323
                                                      CIP

To Our Dear Wives
Betty
and
Doris Ann

Preface

Fear is an experience that crosses human boundaries. It is foreign to neither black nor white, Anglo nor Hispanic, Occidental nor Oriental. It avoids neither poor nor rich. It is daily encountered by both male and female. It takes up residence comfortably with both old and young. It is truly a universal phenomenon.

It is a powerful tool in the hands of manipulators of economics, politics, and religion and it is a basic ingredient of the media industries. The hook of fear is indeed one of the most successful baiting mechanisms known to humanity.

As writers of this book on fear, therefore, we want you to know that we have done our best to look deeply into this universal phenomenon with a view to providing you some insights into the ways in which Christians may seek to deal with it. In this study both of us have sought to bring to bear our research, analysis, and experience gained from over a quarter of a century of teaching, counseling, writing, and spiritual guidance in various parts of the world.

We have made a special effort to communicate to laypersons in this book and have purposely avoided as much of the technical language of our disciplines as possible. But those who are familiar with technical studies should quickly sense that we have made a genuine effort to be as careful as possible with our information and conclusions. In our analysis we have sought to deal with issues that affect both the church and the world and we have not hesitated to deal forthrightly with weaknesses we see in examples of contemporary Christian life.

Our goal is to aid our readers to find some clues for dealing more adequately with threats of fear in their own lives. Our prayer is that our readers will learn how to distinguish between the various types of fear in their own selves and be guided in their quest for spiritual maturity in their pilgrimage of life.

In this work we are indebted to the computer typing pool of The Southern Baptist Theological Seminary and to Broadman Press who have asked us to write the lead book for this new series.

We also wish to thank our dear wives for their patience with us as they lovingly endured the long hours of our work in the preparation of this manuscript. To them this book is gratefully dedicated.

Contents

Contents

Part I
Introduction

1
Fear Not???

Which Is the Real World?

"Once there was a farmer who saw a frightening vision in his barnyard. As he entered, he found the cows peacefully chewing their cuds, the hens clucking to their chicks, a lizard sunning himself without fear. But suddenly there came an incredible transformation. The cows turned into dinosaurs, the chickens to vultures; the lizard became a python, the barnyard a wild threatening jungle.

"The dismaying scene tarried a moment; then it dissolved. Once again the farmer could see his placid cows, the hens and their chicks, the lazy lizard. Ultimately, his terror ebbed. But never again was he to look upon the inhabitants of his barnyard in the way he had before. From that moment on, he was always to wonder which was real, the domestic scene or the primitive wildness."[1]

Perhaps you wonder, too? Perhaps, like the farmer, you are never quite sure whether your world is a safe, domestic scene or a primitive wildness? Could your unsureness have anything to do with your opening this book on the subject of fear? Is it possible that your world frequently feels like a primitive wildness? There may have been a time, long ago, when your "barnyard" was sunlit and peaceful, but then the storms came, tragedy struck, evil strode into your world and took over everything and everybody. From that day to this you may have lived in constant fear, an all-consuming hatred, indifference, apathy, or a confusing and, at times, a terrifying mix of these feelings.

How absurd it must feel to see a chapter title, "Fear Not???" If fear could be overcome by the command, "Fear Not!" who would bother picking up a book about fear? You may have noticed, however, that the title is followed by question marks. "Fear Not???" With the question marks your authors are saying: Who is kidding whom? We are well aware that in the Bible the angels (messengers) of God almost always come with the greeting: "Fear Not!" We know, too, that for us earthbound people, solving the fear problem is not simple.

Fear at Its Worst

Part of the problem may be that not many people are aware of angels saying anything. One person who has lived with fear all of her life wrote a story about it. In the story she finally meets someone who offers real help with her fears. He is a Dragon, rather than an angel, but he offers to be a true friend and travel with her. You would think that this friendship would be an answer to her fears, but. . . . Well, here are some excerpts from the story, showing how it begins and ends.

DRAGONWOOD

I am lost. I don't want to say those words out loud, because when you say words out loud, things get all worse. Only I don't see how things could be much worse than they are right now. But I don't think I ought to take any chances, so I am going to whisper the words, and I promise I won't cry at all.

* * * *

It is so dark in here. The trees are all crowded together like they just finished a dizzy dance, and they are so tall I can't see the sky anymore. I am not sure there even is a sky. I don't much remember skies just now. Anyway, it is very dark in here, and I don't like it, but I have to be very brave. I don't know how to walk in these woods. If I walk real fast, I stumble over roots and rocks or smash into trunks. Sometimes I fall into a muddy pool, and the mud in the bottom of the pool tugs at my feet and tries to eat them before I can pull myself out, and then I am wet and cold. And if I try to walk real slow, then the vines and the mists swallow my face. I don't know how to walk in here. But I won't cry. I think maybe I shouldn't make any noise at all if I can help it. So I won't cry, and I won't walk in circles.

*   *   *   *

What is that ahead? Between the trees. A soft spot of light. Fire? The Dragon! The DRAGON is here! I am not alone anymore!

"Hello. I heard you coming, so I've been waiting for you," the Dragon said in a soft voice. Little puffs of fire came out and warmed the mist away. "Don't get too close to me. You really are all right now. Why don't we sit down and talk for awhile? It's been such a long time since we had a nice talk."

"Do you know where we are?" I asked quickly. "Can you get me out of here?"

"Of course I know where we are. I've been in Dragonwood lots of times. Sometimes when you try to go through it all by yourself you get frightened. It isn't so bad if you have someone with you, someone who knows the trails fairly well. So, calm yourself. Let's just sit and talk for a bit. At least till you get warmer. And the fire from my mouth will let you see things better." So we sat quietly for a few minutes, the Dragon and me, and I wasn't so scared anymore.

*   *   *   *

"There is a way out of the woods," said the Dragon quietly. "When you are ready to leave, I will go with you and show you the way out."

"You'll stay right by me?"

"We will be together."

So we set off. The fire from the Dragon lighted the way better so that we didn't run into trees or rocks or fall into pools. The mist got burned away some so that things were not so dark. The Dragon was bigger and stronger than me, and he knew the way better, so before very long, he got ahead of me. I called out to him.

"Don't be afraid. I'm not going to leave you here in the middle of the woods. When you get scared, you can call out to me. I will talk to you, and when you hear the sound of my voice, you will know that you are not alone."

"Mr. Dragon!" I would yell out when I stumbled over a rock. And he would call back to me, and the sound of his voice would make me feel safe, and I would hurry to catch up with him.

But he went so fast.

I wish the Dragon didn't move so fast through the woods. Even if he knows the way, I wish he would wait for me. I guess he thinks I am too slow, that I should be able to see better, that I am not afraid anymore. I wish he would be right here where I could see him. I wish he would answer my calls. But now I don't see him, and I don't hear his voice. Sometimes he belches a little flame so that I know he is somewhere ahead of me. But it has been dark for a very long time now, and I no longer see the fire, and my voice echoes back to me empty. The mists are heavier, and the trees are closer together, and I am truly alone.

That is what is real. Dragon promises are not real. What is real is the woods and being lost and being alone. Forever.

The author of Dragonwood rides a roller coaster down into the trough of terrifying fear in the forest, up to the crest of hope in the presence and promises of Dragon, and then down again into abandonment and utter hopelessness: ". . . being lost and being alone. Forever."

Dragonwood is a story of despair. The forest of fear may be darker and more dangerous than you have ever known. But do you not recognize some measure of the fear of being alone in Dragonwood? Have you not had some hints of the dread of losing contact with a big, strong, and kindly guide as you seek to find your way through the dangers of life? The story of Dragonwood happens to most people in growing up. It is the story of little children growing up among adults who are alternately gentle and cruel, welcoming and rejecting, protecting and punishing without provocation. Sometimes the adults are trapped in the seesaw of being sober and drunk, but other times they are sober, religious, and respectable in their public life while violent, evil, and unnatural in the privacy of the home. One's home may become a Dragonwood and fear become one's daily bread in situations such as these. Fear can become the air you breath, the eyes through which you see everyone else, and the feeling that penetrates your moods, your daydreams, your nightmares, and your behaviors as well.

For some, Dragonwood is their story. It is true to life in its loneliness—in loneliness that is black with broken promises. The loneliness of Dragonwood allows no sunspots of hope. It is the loneliness of a person who is more in love with death than with life. Apathy fills the soul. Dragonwood people are never far from the awareness of a dark, cold, nonrational, and totally unresponsive reality within. The apathy zone is potentially present in everyone. It is hidden, impenetrable, sealed-off stuff of the soul out of which ooze stupid, self-defeating behaviors, self-blame, and rage at the world within, as well as deeply hidden resentment of the world outside.

The possibility of love and life stir only shame and repulsion in Dragonwood captives. Being around people who believe in the power of love raises in such a soul a wall, felt first by others in words and then in silence. When you believe yourself lost in Dragonwood forever, you feel neither gratitude nor admiration for your would-be helpers. You threaten them with your unspoken disdain of life and love. As for God, those who live in Dragonwood have received the mystic vision, but it is not a vision of light and love. Elie Wiesel records the vision as it came to a teenage Jewish boy in Auschwitz watching his elders pray:

> This day I had ceased to plead. I was no longer capable of lamentation. On the contrary, I felt very strong. I was the accuser, God the accused. My eyes were open and I was alone—terribly alone in a world without God and without man. Without love or mercy. I had

ceased to be anything but ashes, yet I felt myself to be stronger than the Almighty, to whom my life had been tied for so long. I stood amid that praying congregation, observing it like a stranger.[2]

The Vicious Cycle of Fear

You can trace the journey into Dragonwood most clearly by watching what happens to infants neglected by their parenting adults. First the infant cries. The discomfort of being wet, cold, and hungry stirs a mighty protest. A wall of rage springs up between the infant and the whole world. Let the infant's needs be met and the wall crumbles. Tenderness and attachment take over. The infant's energy is still moving toward and not away from the adults.

Let neglect continue unrelieved and the infant will change. Crying will change to whimpers. The protests will be over. The baby will turn to the wall, become listless, unresponsive, disinterested in the bottle and in people. Energy is still moving toward potential caregivers, however, in spite of all the signs to the contrary. For when care is restored, the little one will slowly, but surely, return to the ways of tender loving care. The return journey comes through the painful territory of agitation and protest, but the child does come home again to love.

The pit of hell is deeper yet. Without the healing presence of genuine care and with increasing degrees of malnutrition, neglect, and abuse, the infant moves into the third level of despair, the level of apathy. A child may brighten in apathy. Behavior may become less troublesome to adults, but only because the little one has learned to play the game of "as if." The child lives "as if" all were well, but inside all the energy is moving away from the outside world, away from life and love. The child, even as an infant, may well fall in love with death.

Protest—Depression—Apathy: These are three levels of lostness of a neglected, lonely soul. The process is the same whether in infant or adult. These are degrees of darkness in

Dragonwood, degrees of intensity of fear. The deeper one goes into the Dragonwood forest the more constant is the companionship of fear. The less a person hopes for escape, the more difficult the task of a loving Dragon who would like to show the lonely, fear-ridden person the way out. The more incredible, yes even laughable, becomes the announcement of the messengers of God: "Fear Not!"

Biblical Realism About Fear

Before you close the door on the possibility that God is seeking those who are lost in Dragonwood, however, consider what the Bible says about fear and loneliness. As you read the pages of the Bible with your mind tuned to the subject of fear, you will discover that it is one of those pervading themes that underlies many of the stories and the messages from Genesis through Revelation. Fear is like a yellow thread that seems, at least, to haunt the settings of the inspired texts.

Dealing with fear and the feelings of aloneness and alienation is a great concern for the biblical writers. Elisha's servant trembled when he saw the little city of Dothan surrounded by the great Syrian army. I wonder what he thought when Elisha said, "Fear not" (2 Kings 6:16)? He must have felt like he was in the middle of Dragonwood. Likewise there is little doubt that the disciples were gripped by a similar terror when the boat in which they were riding was being pounded by the storm, was filling with water, and was about to sink, while Jesus was peacefully asleep in the stern. What do you imagine they thought when Jesus awoke and said, "Why do you fear?" (Mark 4:40).

But there is more to the idea of fear in the Bible than such obvious references. How do you read the story of Adam and Eve in the first book of the Bible? What do you imagine were the feelings of Adam when God came walking in the cool part of the day calling: "Adam, where are you?" (Gen. 3:9). Do you think that Adam was feeling much like singing a song about walking together with God in the Garden? Do you imagine that at that point he was ready to chant, We can talk as good friends while we walk? Do you think he would have felt comfortable stretching his hand out to God at that point? Any advice from an observer that he really did not need to fear God at that moment would probably have sounded like a hollow echo to Adam. He and Eve had disobeyed God and there was no question that they were just a little bit worried—probably just a little more than terrified of what would happen next.

The story tells us that the couple did not have to wait very long to find out whether Adam had legitimate grounds for his fear. God came looking and calling for His erring children and Adam, in his haste to defend himself, uncovered his disobedience (3:10). Unbeknown to him, he blurted out his problem. He truly spilled the beans! The couple's attempted justification of their actions by each blaming someone else hardly sat well with God. They soon discovered in that incident what many people come to realize when they are out of sync with God—namely, the weight of a gripping experience of fear.

For us as writers to tell you, therefore, that there are no reasons to fear would hardly represent either experience or the Bible correctly. Moreover, it would scarcely be the point of this present book. Instead it is the goal of this study to deal forthrightly both with the reality of the human experience of fear and the insights from the Bible which may help you to deal more effectively with your task of living in a world that is generally marked by fear.

"Fear" and "Fear Not"

The Bible takes fear seriously. Indeed, some books of the Bible may tend to lead us through a strange path which both engenders fear and counsels against fear. Such is the style of the last book of the Bible—Revelation. To read Revelation in a meaningful manner is always to have in mind both those whom John suggests ought to be terrified (Rev. 11:11) and those whom he considers should not be frightened. The strange and weird images that explode from the pages of that apocalyptic vision were hardly intended to be read as stanzas in a sweet cradle song. The "Fear not" of Revelation 1:17 was not intended for everyone, but such advice is directed only to those who have recognized and are willing to follow the One who died and now is alive forever (v. 18).

The biblical message is, in fact, intended to bring confidence to God's people. When John, who himself represented authentic Christians, saw in chapter 1 a spine-tingling vision of Christ (vv. 12-16), he was terrified and fell stunned at the feet of Christ (v. 17). As we might expect, the figure of Christ in that vision told John not to fear. This pattern of vision and word is not very different from the many appearances of the angel of the Lord in the Old Testament. The descendants of Abraham trembled at the thought of seeing the angel of the Lord, as in the case of Gideon (Judg. 6:22). The Israelites earnestly hoped that if they saw that angel they would also hear the comforting words, "Peace to you" or "Fear not" (for example, v. 23).

But the biblical perspective is not quite that simple because in addition to "fear not" there is a parallel message which calls on God's people to fear God. This message of fearing God is also present in the Book of Revelation. For example, as the angel carried the precious gospel between heaven and earth, he sternly thundered to the dwellers of this world, "Fear God!" (14:7).

To fear or not to fear? That is the biblical and life-centered question around which this present study revolves. It is a tension at the very heart of the holy Scriptures and is inherent within the struggle of every human who searches for meaning and at-homeness.

My God! My God! Why Have You Abandoned Me?

To be human means to struggle with fear and aloneness. To be honest is not to settle for easy answers about fear, but it is to wrestle with the mystery of the divine-human relationship. To begin to deal with the depth of this mystery one needs to be reminded of the crucial story in the gospels where Jesus was hanging on the cross. In that crisis hour Jesus cried out "My God! My God! Why have you abandoned me?" (Mark 15:34; Matt. 27:46).* What do you make of those words? Have they shocked you?

Whatever they mean, the Gospel writers thought they were incredibly important. How do you know that? Whenever the New Testament writers take pains to write something not merely in Greek but in Aramaic or Hebrew and then also include a Greek translation of those words, you can generally count on the fact that those words were significant for the early church.

Well, if those words are so significant, what do they mean? Yes, they are a quotation out of the Old Testament. Indeed, they are the opening words of Psalm 22. Concerning Jesus' quotation here, some Christians are quick to remind you that Jesus probably lived with the Old Testament and knew it pretty well. That suggestion seems quite likely. Some are equally quick to point out that this psalm seems to end more positively than it begins and, therefore, they suggest that even though Jesus' words seem to be shocking, they really point to His ultimate victory. Now there is no doubt that He won a victory. But, I doubt very much whether that is what is meant by those words. Jesus usually said what He meant, unless He was purposely telling parables. Jesus was not speaking in parables at this point! Accordingly, could He not have said, "I am winning the victory," if that is what He meant? Was the cross the place where Jesus became uncommonly subtle? Or do we out of fear for ourselves and our theologies *try to protect Jesus* from the human emotion of fear?

Are you really willing to affirm the incarnation faith you glibly confess as a Christian? Or do you compromise your confession? When Jesus was on earth was He just God, as the early heretics used to say? Or was he really the God-man, who fully experienced humanness *without sin?* Could it be possible that He experienced terrifying fear? Think what that might mean? After all, in Hebrews we are told that we do not have in Jesus an uninvolved high priest but one who has been through life and is able to empathize with us even though He did not sin like us (4:15-16).

The Question of Fear Today

When you think about fear, what does it mean to you? When you hear the words "Fear not!" what do they mean? Fear is surely one of humanity's strongest emotions. Any analysis of television commercials quickly confirms the fact that advertisers like to use human fears to promote their products. And what about politicians? Fear enables them to gain their objectives, whether it be through truth or subterfuge. To be fair, one must also ask the question of the use of fear by church leaders. When is the use of fear legitimate and when does it become a manipulative vehicle for achieving personal goals?

Of the presence of fear in the Bible there is no doubt. It is a collection of books which openly talks about fear and it does not avoid dealing with the difficult aspects of human feelings and emotions. Because the biblical writers genuinely presupposed that human emotions were created by God, there was no reason to exclude them from the concern of God or from consideration in the Bible. The very opposite is, in fact, the case. The biblical writers did not grow up in a fashionable era which covered reality with lace or which perfumed fear with mouthwash. Nor did the biblical writers consider it appropriate to limit their discussions to a straight-laced Victorian propriety which sought to bury such aspects of the human emotions. Nor did the biblical writers accept the free-wheeling style of so-called contemporary epicureans who think that carefree self-indulgence is a cure for the pangs of fear. The biblical writers were honest about actions and emotions. They defined the world and human activity by the yardstick of God and only by that measure was fear to be correctly perceived. The Bible is a book that calls us to fear and not to fear! Between those two commands hang the tensions of human life.

Part II
The Power to Curse or to Bless

2

Repression or Confession?

Repression Is Bad for Your Health

The faces of fear that you saw in chapter 1 may be unfamiliar to you. If so, it may be that you are repressing the worst of your fears. Repressed feelings are bad for your health. Repression is a process of blocking out of conscious awareness both the facts and feelings that are frightening. What makes repression dangerous is that it happens without your knowing it. The process of intending to control unacceptable feelings is called suppression. Suppression is done on purpose, knowing full well that you are doing so. You can choose what you will do with feelings that you suppress. But it is not so with repression. What is repressed is out of conscious control. Repressed fears are hidden from view but not stripped of their destructive power. They are buried for the time being, but they are not dead.

What happens to the ugly, repulsive, and frightening stuff that you cope with by repression? It becomes your private dump, your hidden hell. What happens, then, when you try to live on top of buried garbage as if it were not there? Like sewer gas, it makes you nervous, uncomfortable, and troubled even before you are fully conscious of the source of the odor. Occasionally, like a smoking volcano, it erupts with terrifying force and tragic consequences.

Facing Fears: The First Step

Everyone relies on repression to dispose of frightening feelings some of the time. Some people rely on repression all the time. But there is a better way. You do not have to live nervously on top of a garbage dump nor dangerously on the rim of a volcano. The better way is told in a story that is centuries old, yet as modern as today.

The story is Dante's *Divine Comedy*. It is about a Pilgrim in the prime of life who is lost in a dark forest. Seeing a sunlit mountaintop and knowing that to climb it would mean to be free at last, Pilgrim sets foot on the trail only to be met by the beasts of the forest. Backing down as fast as possible, Pilgrim is again lost in the forest, this time with no hope of getting out alive.

About to panic, Pilgrim sees someone coming. It is none other than Virgil, the wise old man who was Pilgrim's favorite teacher and guide in youth. Virgil offers to guide Pilgrim safely to the mountaintop, to the fulfillment of Pilgrim's highest hopes and dreams. Pilgrim is overwhelmed with surprise and joy. But joy is short-lived. Virgil says, "Your journey must be down a different road . . . if ever you hope to leave this wilderness"—a road that leads through hell. When Virgil's words sink in, Pilgrim gives up on the journey.

Virgil then tells a story of happenings in heaven. Beatrice, who was Pilgrim's first love, who died in her early twenties, was sent from heaven to ask Virgil to guide Pilgrim to the gates of Paradise, at which point Beatrice, herself, would become Pilgrim's guide.

Pilgrim is now ready to face anything in order to be with Beatrice on the journey. So with Virgil close beside, Pilgrim passes through the gates of hell to explore the dark realms of human degradation. Dante is clear that his story is about the choices people make in life. Dante's *Hell* is about the buried garbage in everyone.

More surprises await Pilgrim at every turn on the terrifying trail through hell. One discovery is that people in hell are living as they chose to live on earth. Their pain is self-inflicted. It is not consciously chosen, however. It is the pain that follows repression. It is pain that cries out for confession yet is only buried more deeply. Pilgrim discovers also that people get more evil the deeper he goes into Lower Hell. The region becomes more cold. People become more and more isolated from each other. Finally the travelers come to the pit of hell where they find Satan frozen in a lake of ice. They make their escape to find that having faced the worst, they are free from hell's terrors and full of energy for the climb up the mountain of maturity (Purgatory) toward godlikeness in love (Paradise).

So, here is the clue. The better way is to enter your own hell and to explore the dark and dangerous realm beneath and within you. Dante understood that to be freed from your fears, you must face them. Facing fears is the first step in confessing them. It involves confessing them to yourself and to God. Once you face and confess your fears you discover that you have more power for your life's journey. Things get better for you rather than worse. The energy you were spending to keep the gateway into your private hell closed and locked is now free for growing, for enjoying life, and for caring for others.

Two Portraits of Repression and Confession

The biblical stories of Saul and David vividly picture the contrast between repression and confession in a person's life. King Saul is a fascinating example of a complex person enmeshed in repressed and explosive feelings. As Samuel grew old, the people of Israel demanded a king like their neighbors. Saul was a winsome young man. He was handsome and stalwart in appearance (1 Sam. 9:2). He seemed to be humble (v. 21) and the power and spirit of God was seen in his life (10:6-13). Who could have guessed that a boiling volcano was to erupt later in his life?

As he assumed the crown, fatal flaws became evident in Saul. He began to think that his position of king gave him special privileges. On one occasion Saul even took to himself the rights and responsibilities of sacrifice that belonged to Samuel (13:9-11). Saul's anxiety about losing his army prompted him to act as though the timing of events was in his hand. He seems to have supposed that Israel's destiny before God turned on his personal, impetuous actions (vv. 11-12). He became transfixed with the idea of his own self-worth, but his impulsiveness led instead to judgment. As a result, Saul became a boiling caldron, a person haunted by Samuel's words that God had selected someone else—a man after his "own heart"—to whom the kingdom would be given (v. 14).

Israel's enemies were a constant thorn in Saul's flesh and the battles with those enemies became the gradual means by which God's inevitable judgment was worked out. Jonathan, Saul's heir apparent, unaware of his father's senseless curse on those who ate before the end of the battle (14:24), became an innocent victim of his own father's stupid attempt at controlling the troops and engendering loyalty (vv. 27-30). Then, Saul's disobedient taking of plunder in the battle with the Amalekites and his pious talk of sacrifice (15:14-15) led to Samuel's exasperated words of judgment upon Saul (vv. 16-29), and finally to a face-to-face encounter with Israel's failure-prone king (v. 35). The inevitable dirge continued with Saul's inability to handle Goliath and the Philistine challenge. Then Saul's solution, to trade his daughter for a successful Israelite champion, brought David, his successor, into the very palace precincts.

The stories in the Bible which follow, concerning the encounters between Saul and David, provide a marvelous study in contrasts on the themes of repression and confession. Saul, the one who possessed kingly power, is portrayed as an inconsistent, troubled, old man. His deep-rooted fears of losing the kingdom turned him into a seething volcano which was constantly ready to spew its evil destruction over anyone that appeared the least supportive of his enemy whom he wanted dead. David, on the other hand, is pictured as a courageous young man of integrity who inspired others to follow the way of authenticity, and who, although he feared Saul's devices, refused to use any advantage to harm the king.

The biblical stories unveil situations in which people could not help but compare David and Saul, and the comparisons made Saul boil with fearful hate (18:6-9). David's soothing lyre and Saul's threatening spear are symbols of the inner peace and the burning anger of each man (vv. 10-11). Saul's uncontrolled reactions were the result of fearing David because the people could see the difference between them (vv. 12-16). Saul did not keep his promise to give his eldest daughter in marriage to David, but when Saul saw that his younger daughter Michal loved David, he schemed to use that love to bring about David's death. David overcame the scheme and Saul's fear of him grew worse (vv. 17-29).

Try as they might, Jonathan, Michal, and David could not seem to soften the haunting fear that troubled the king. Consequently, Saul's fear caused turmoil in his own family (1 Sam. 19—20). Fear tragically made it impossible for him to understand the feelings of his own son and daughter, to say nothing of the feelings of his son-in-law.

But Saul's problem was far deeper than family relations. He had once been an accepted servant of God, and he knew what it meant to be approved. Like most humans he was also subject to failure. His problem was that he did not handle his failures adequately. Instead of dealing forthrightly with his own failures before God, he focused his attention on somebody else, blaming and hounding another servant of God. As a result, he became imprisoned in his own fears and he developed into a servant of evil rather than good. So low did he sink that he even commanded the priests of the tabernacle to be executed in order to satisfy the anger which erupted from his fear (1 Sam. 21:1 to 22:19). The boiling volcano of unmanaged fear birthed Saul, the monster.

In some respects, David was tempted by the power of kingship much like his predecessor, Saul. Indeed, David's sins may be viewed by some Christians as deeper and more devastating than those of Saul. Yet the Bible speaks of David as being a man after God's heart (1 Sam. 13:14; Acts 13:22). You could hardly call him sinless or see him as a model for young people today. While Saul is a tragic figure, however, the tragedies of David are seen quite differently in the Bible. If you are wondering, "What accounts for this difference?" you may agree that one clue to David's acceptance is to be found in Dante's Pilgrim. In the midst of his hurts and fear Pilgrim was willing to recognize his own weakness and accept help from outside himself.

Like Saul, David in his youth showed great promise of integrity. Justifiably, one could argue as the story proceeds that David should have acted against Saul. Indeed, he could easily have killed Saul both at Engedi (1 Sam. 24) and at Hachilah (1 Sam. 26). After all, Saul had consistently treated him unfairly and had even declared him to be an enemy of the state, to be taken either dead or alive. But David refused to follow the vengeful pattern of the fear-ridden king, even though he and his small, faithful band had to flee for their lives time and again from the forces of Saul. In the integrity of his being David had covenanted before God that he would not gain the kingdom by killing the king, even though that route could have meant a quick way to power.

But David was not totally consistent in his patterns of action. Like Saul he revealed major flaws in his life. Between the two incidents of Engedi and Hachilah his anger was kindled against the ungrateful Nabal. David was ready to split him open with the sword (1 Sam. 25). Abigail, the sensitive wife of Nabal, however, kept David from a senseless murder by reminding him that God was able to deal with injustice (vv. 23-31). The willingness of David to listen to the wise advice of others and to change his mind (vv. 32-35) is undoubtedly a key to what made David able to deal wisely with his weaknesses and sins.

David was also a man of strategy. He could hardly be accused of failing to plan out the well-being of Israel or the exaltation of God. One of his first acts after being made king over the whole of Israel was to capture Jerusalem and bring the ark of the covenant to the city. His goal was to build a house or Temple for God. But the death of Uzzah (2 Sam. 6:6-11) and the word of the prophet Nathan (7:1-17) changed the great dream of David. David was a man of power like Saul, but when God and His prophets got in the way of David's strategy, David was willing to accept a change in the process.

Perhaps nowhere is that reality clearer than in the story of David's sin with Bathsheba. In that story David, the man of power, committed adultery with the wife of one of his loyal officers. Try as he might, David could not suppress his sin by legitimizing Bathsheba's pregnancy through the recall of Uriah. When David's strategy failed, he turned to a convenient plot which would achieve the death of Uriah so that David could marry Bathsheba (2 Sam. 11). But God did not allow David to bury his sin in that scheme either. Nathan uncovered David's strategy and condemned him (12:1-12). Now David had the option: either silence the prophet or confess the sin. Unlike Saul, David could not think of killing God's representative. Clearly, David had known too much about God to elect the way of self-justification. He chose the way of confession. Even though he lived with turmoil in his family (2 Sam. 13—18), David reestablished the integrity of his own life (2 Sam. 12:13). Confession is the biblical way of dealing with buried fear. It is the way of confronting the dark side of your life, the means of neutralizing the hell within you.

You are not wise, however, to try to travel through your own hell alone. You need to go with a guide who has been there often before and who, best of all, travels with the authority of heaven. The best of guides is the Spirit of God working through one who drinks deeply of the Spirit's wisdom. The courage for the journey is called "coming clean with yourself," "joining the human race," "being honest with yourself before God." By whatever phrase you speak of it, you are doing the work that Scripture calls confession.

When Your Inner Hell Is Hard to Face

Returning to the story of Dante's *Hell*, Pilgrim found two realms, an Upper Hell and a Lower Hell. The people in Upper Hell had given themselves over to self-indulgence. Theirs were the sins of lust, gluttony, greed, and wrath. They were victims of their own choices. They lived in bleak, windswept, desertlike places or in swampy muck, under cold and dirty rain, hail, and snow. They exploited one another and hated each other, but they were not totally alone. They were connected with the human family, if only in selfish ways.

In Lower Hell the scene changed radically. Landscapes gave way to a walled city and the screaming Furies; to the stench of open tombs, deep ravines with bands of roaming devils, nests of snakes, souls in flames, and, finally, a lake of ice. Hate became violent, envy turned evil, and pride was cold, calculating, cruel, and murderous. People were totally isolated from each other, full of rage and blaming, betraying family members, friends, country, and God.

Dante saw things going on in the realm of repression that are hard to face. He saw the impulses of the body to be far less deadly than the pride and envy of the soul. He saw the clergy and other religious people in Lower Hell more often than in Upper Hell. Theirs were the sins of the soul more often than sins of the body. Yet vast numbers of religious folk today are quick to see sin in the impulses of the body, such as sex and aggression, in passions and appetites for food and drink, but are blind to the sins of hate and violence, envy and pride, especially when these behaviors are veiled in religious zeal.

How easy it is to blind yourself to your pride, for example, in your zeal to be humble. Hear the story of the rabbi who, on the Day of Atonement was standing in front of the congregation reciting the liturgy. He was beating his breast, and crying, "O Lord, I am nothing. O Lord, I am nothing. O Lord, I am nothing."

The cantor picked up the refrain and said, "O Lord, I am nothing. O Lord, I am nothing. O Lord, I am nothing."

Just then the janitor who was at the back of the sanctuary spontaneously cried out, "O Lord, I am nothing. O Lord, I am nothing. O Lord, I am nothing."

The rabbi turned to the cantor and said, "Look at him who thinks he is nothing."[1]

Do you recognize yourself in the rabbi? Do you see the irony in accusing the janitor of pride out of your own unrecognized pride of position? Can you laugh at yourself as you see your impulse to be harsh and critical of the janitor who spontaneously entered into the true meaning of public confession?

In a more serious vein, do you understand what is going on inside a person who is prideful while confessing humility, hateful in the name of love, deceitful in professing truth, making war in the name of peace, or betraying with a kiss? Do you know how easy it is to conceal pride in the very act of confessing it? Confession is a cure for repression, but even confession can be corrupted by forces of which you are not aware.

Naming the Enemy Inside: Tyrannical Conscience

The name of the villain in your hidden self may be tyrannical conscience. Conscience is not the court of highest appeal. Conscience is easily corrupted. You can let your conscience be your guide only so long as you know that "God is greater than our conscience" (1 John 3:20). The difference is easy to tell. "God is love" (1 John 4:16), but tyrannical conscience is a tormentor.

The signs of a tyrannical conscience at work are two: the most obvious is behavior that torments others. The more subtle is tormenting yourself and unwittingly falling into behaviors that are self-defeating. Underlying these tell-tale signs are the feelings of shame and guilt.

Internalized ideals are feelings of obligation or "ought." Shame comes in many colors: feeling disgraced, ridiculous, humiliated. You may feel chagrined, embarrassed, or mortified. You may say, for example, "I could have died!" When shame becomes ingrained in a person's life, you may say that the person is shy, bashful, overly modest, or too self-conscious.

Internalized prohibitions consist of taboos or the feeling, "I ought not:" I ought not do this or that; I ought not speak this or that feeling; I ought not even feel this or that. To feel the forbidden feeling is to experience guilt. The word *guilt* comes from the Teutonic root, *Schuld*, meaning debt. Deep in the soul of a guilt-ridden person is a sense of debt, an expectation that as a debtor one will have to pay—one deserves punishment.

Feelings of guilt may not be experienced as much, but they often show up as feelings of obligation and duty. Guilt masks itself in feelings of blame when blame is not the issue. Guilt may be covered by feelings of responsibility for what is some-one else's problem. You may feel fated to suffer or to pay for choices others have made. You can hear the echo of guilt in phrases such as, "I just had to," "I was bound to do it," "I felt compelled," "it was my duty," "someone had to pay," or "I had it coming." So guilt refers to the violation of rules or taboos laid down by others; shame refers to the failure to measure up to standards or expectations that you have internalized within yourself. Guilt often triggers shame as shame may be fused with guilt. The two functions of conscience merge and overlap most of the time. The distinction between shame and guilt proves helpful mainly in recognizing tyrannical conscience for what it is.

Tyrannical conscience, then, describes a conscience that runs amok. It is mad with the desire to attack. It is irrational and totally unrealistic in its assessment of a situation. Con-science is meant to protect you, but a tyrannical conscience defeats and sometimes destroys you. A deformed conscience berates you like a raging parent who is furious with a child. It lashes out with irrational accusations not only against your deeds, but also against the very thoughts you think. It makes you feel that it is not safe to admit to yourself your genuine needs as a human being.

Give a tyrannical conscience voice and it may scream: "How could you think such a thing? But that's what you are, isn't it? You're an animal, that's what you are! You're coarse, vulgar, low-down, dirty, and vicious! Just look at you. What a pre-tense! Shame on you! You will pay dearly for this!"

In contrast, a sound conscience admonishes you like a caring friend. Its advice is realistic and is offered in a spirit of good-will. For instance, it may say, "Hey, wait a minute. Let's think about that a bit. Your wishes are perfectly normal, but suppose you indulge those wishes? What will be the consequences? I know you have worked hard, and you didn't have much as a kid. Yes, you are entitled to enjoy yourself now. But do you really want to risk your family and your career and the rewards of making the contribution you are now making for a bit of self-indulgence?"

Tyrannical conscience wears many masks, but one unmistakable clue is cruelty. Such a conscience makes you harsh with yourself and others; impatient with your weaknesses as well as theirs. It makes you intolerant of failures, especially when rules or moral codes have been broken. The voice of a tyrannical conscience is intimidating. It demands that you conform not to your own good sense or to the high ethic of love, but to the self-destructive rules and taboos that are driving you.

The Christian's Struggle and Romans 7

Scarcely is there a more vivid illustration of the force of a tyrannical conscience than the much-debated words of Romans 7. Paul, the Jewish rabbi, had lived under the tyranny of a conscience that had been molded by a commitment that involved absolute obedience to the law. In his quest for peace from the fear of disobedience to the law, the law became for him a ball and chain that gripped him with a sense of hopelessness (vv. 10-11). It was not the law, however, that was his problem. The law he acknowledged came from God (v. 7). The problem was his own life and the reality of sin (v. 8).

No matter how he tried to obey the commands of God, he could not seem to get beyond the harsh requirements of the law and his own human sinfulness (vv. 13-14). The law was like a stern superself forcing him constantly to recognize the defeated nature of his own humanity. In utter helplessness he cried for an understanding of himself (v. 15). Why did he do what he detested? And why was he unable to do what he wanted to do? His conclusion could be nothing else than that he was a divided self (v. 20)!

But such was not Paul's problem merely as a Jewish rabbi. The fact is that he was able to say the same thing about himself as a Christian. Indeed, the entire argument of Romans 7 is written not in the past tense but in the present tense. Now many interpreters of Paul are absolutely vehement in their protests against this text being used to represent Paul as a Christian. They argue that when Paul experienced new life he ceased all anxieties or concerns with respect to his life. About all we can say to such theology is that, when Paul became a Christian, he did not cease being a human. What he did do, however, is truly accept his humanness and the marvelous grace of God in his life.

Nevertheless, there was a major difference for him as a Christian. He could never deliver himself from himself to be sure. In the manner of the Greeks, therefore, he might have been tempted to suicide as the ultimate means of escape. Remember his question: "Who will deliver me?" (v. 24). In Christ, however, he refused to accept the Greek answer of escape. He found, instead, another way. That way was the process of coming to terms with himself—the acceptance of the dark side of himself (v. 25). Splitness is primarily troublesome when it is repressed and not brought out into the open. When, however, it is acknowledged and forced into the light of the grace of God in confession, there is a wonderful sense of freedom that results. As Paul argued so forcefully: when one is open to God, condemnation is removed (8:1). Thus, even though our bodies do not always respond to the will of Christ because of sin, when Christ is in us, we are alive to righteousness in the power of the resurrection of Christ Jesus (vv. 10-11).

In this acceptance by Christ we are able to deal with our fears concerning sin, lack of integrity or power, and even death (vv. 12-13). We are also able to call God by the intimate, accepting name of "Father" because the Spirit of God living in us confirms in us our acceptance as children of God (vv. 14-16).

Our task then is not to retreat into the valley of conformity with the fears, anxieties, and activities of the world. Our God-given responsibility is to follow the pattern of Christ no matter what hardship such following may bring (v. 17). In obeying the Spirit's genuine leading and in following the model of Christ, Paul discovered a new sense of freedom, integrity, power, support, and direction (vv. 26-39). Moreover, it was his prayer in using the pronoun "we" that all Christians might discover the same transforming power and love of God in Christ Jesus *our* Lord!

Confession as Coming Clean

Paul's struggle with his divided self shows that the first step in dealing with fears is to confess them rather than to repress them. Confession is "coming clean" about the things that trigger your shame and guilt. This confessing is essential for spiritual well-being. A healthy conscience is a reliable guide to "coming clean," but a tyrannical conscience must itself be confessed as a dangerous form of spiritual bondage rather than be obeyed as the voice of God. A tyrannical conscience allows nothing more than a pseudoconfession.

Pseudoconfession is everywhere condemned in the Gospels, and Jesus' response to sinners turns the rules of a tyrannical conscience upside down. Jesus was strangely kind to an adulterous women who was caught in the very act of immorality (John 8:3-11). A similar attitude is shown in Luke's Gospel. A reputedly sinful woman entered the home of Simon the Pharisee, wept over the feet of Jesus, wiped them with her hair, and anointed them with ointment (7:38). While Simon, in effect, condemned both her and the openness of the Lord to such a person, Jesus was forgiving. The humble sinners in the Gospel stories, just like the poor and ill-treated of society, were told by Jesus about God's forgiving power and the gift of peace in their lives (see vv. 48-50).

The situation was radically different in Jesus' encounters with the so-called righteous of society. The scribes and Pharisees who were driven by tyrannical conscience, were labeled "hypocrites" in Matthew's Gospel (Matt. 23). It is similar in Luke's magnificent stories of the Pharisee and the publican (Luke 18:9-14), the good Samaritan (10:25-37), the sinful woman (7:36-50), the prodigal son (15:11-32), and the rich man and Lazarus (16:19-31). In these stories most of the people who appear to have been righteous and proper, according to the usual standards of judgment, were severely criticized by Jesus because they also evidenced a self-righteousness which made them unable to sense the wonderful grace of the self-giving God. As has been stated elsewhere:

> Hypocrisy is an ever present cancer that feeds among religious people. It is not something that was confined to the synagogue and Jewish pietists. It haunts the halls of the church as well. Our Lord knew how to condemn unrighteousness and warned us not to condemn others quickly or easily. Instead, He soberly promised us that the way we judge others would become the pattern for the way we would be judged (see Matt. 7:1-2).[2]

Whether Dante was right, therefore, in picturing two levels in hell—one for the sinners of self-indulgence and wrath, and one for those who are given to pride and self-righteousness—will probably not be clear on this side of the judgment seat of God. But one thing we can say for sure is that, when we face the God of heaven and earth, that God is not going to have a different perspective than the Jesus of the Gospels. If the Gospel stories are any indication of God's attitudes toward self-righteousness, then the warning of the poet Dante certainly needs to be heeded. Accordingly, we who may claim to be righteous need to recognize the strange faces of evil in our own lives. We need to name the enemies in ourselves that seek to enslave us.

Confession as Coming Home

Another face of confession is "coming home." It is "coming home" to your body, to your ego needs, to your relationship needs, and to your privacy needs. It is making peace with your humanness, relaxing your need to be a "super person," and enjoying the simple joys of being alive.

Confession in these terms is affirmation. It is a deep inner affirmation of God's gift of a human body. Affirming your needs for food and shelter helps you to find the line between needs and wants. Your wants may lure you into greed, and greed certainly calls for "coming clean"; but your needs bind you to one another and to God. As needs, you can celebrate your sexual feelings and your sexual powers. It is slavery to wants, however, that allows sexual experience to lure you into self-indulgence.

Similarly, ego needs are both gift and self-deception. You ground yourself in the good soil of psychic life when you affirm the goodness of your ego needs. Ego needs keep you from getting stuck in self-doubt or in belittling and discounting your strengths. Ego needs stimulate common sense and produce the good fruit of self-esteem without which you have little genuine care to give to others. Only when ego needs get caught up in egotism do they feed self-centeredness, self-absorption, self-praise, vanity, and arrogance. When egotism takes over, "coming clean" is an urgent emergency treatment. As self-esteem grows, however, you may rejoice in your ego needs and know that such rejoicing is a confession of the goodness of God. Such confession is a celebration, a coming home to God's purposes for your growth.

Relationship needs are real as well. Too little risking in relationship with other people can shrivel a soul. Too much people time, whether in working or in partying, can shallow a soul and stunt its growth. Privacy needs and the needs for rest and reflection balance the needs for play and for sharing life with others. Here, too, confession arises out of awareness both of the imbalance in your life, and of the gift of people with whom to share your life. Confession becomes the pulse of the soul beating out a rhythm of "coming clean" and "coming home."

Confession as Fear and Trembling

As you exercise your spiritual muscles in confession—both in sorrow for sin and in affirmation of the gift of life—you grow strong enough to enter the experience of confession as fear and trembling. The rhythm of the soul collapses into a spiritual dysrhythmia when you lean over the railing of life and look into the Void. As planet Earth moves in empty space around the sun, so earthbound people move through life in a capsule of awareness surrounded by Emptiness, Aloneness, Void.

Most people will do anything to avoid looking into the Void. The capsule of everyday awareness is a fragile thing, however. Sometimes it cracks open when you are present at a birth; often when you face death, whether your own or anothers. What is called "nervous breakdown" or "mental illness" may mask a glimpse of the Void. To look into the Void is to know utter Terror, Horror, Abandonment, Emptiness, Evil. Fear becomes Absolute. Typically you attempt to look away at once. You try to forget what you saw. You tense up. You plunge into business or booze, or both. You tighten your grip on the piece of life you can control. You are likely either to conform rigidly to the rules of society or to defy its conventions openly. In either case you are driven by the need to forget what you saw when you leaned over the balcony of the everyday and looked down into the Void.

Confession now is raw fear and trembling. Confession draws you back to the balcony again and again. You cannot forget for long what you have seen. Life's journey is laced with an inner terror that will not go away. The soul cannot be sedated for long. Your inmost self wakens again and again to the awe-full reality that you stumbled upon when first you saw the Void.

Whether you have a religious orientation or not, you cry out for someone to be in the Void. Your cries may be wordless or they may be so loud that everyone around you knows that something is wrong with you. Most people cry out mainly to one another, trying to get someone to comfort them, to reassure them, to tell them the Void is not really Empty, that Evil is merely the temporary absence of Good. Others are heroic. They stand trembling on the balcony and continue crying into the Void, fascinated and terrified by the mystery. They try to force the hand of whatever gods there may be. Their pride is magnificent!

Happy are you when you fail to find reassurance whether in standing firm or in running away. Happy are you when your pride crumbles and you give up the heroic struggle to force the hand of God. Happy are you when your strength gives out and you can no longer run. For then the conditions are right for the Void to yield to the Presence of the Holy One.

In the Presence of God, fear is not dissolved; it is tranformed into Wisdom. "Fear Not!" reassures you that you have been met by a Presence rather than the Void. "Fear the Lord your God!" transforms both your fears and your inmost self with the courage of hope and perfect love. The Uncanny—yes! The Awe-ful—yes! Absolute Mystery—yes! But Aloneness—no! Emptiness—no! Evil—no! The Demonic is overcome in the Divine. The Void becomes bearable in the Presence.

And what about confession? Confession continues to be fear and trembling. The fear is the "Fear of the Lord" and the trembling is "Amazing Grace." The Holy One is beyond the Void and also within your soul. The "beyond" calls for fear and the "within" calls for trembling. The response is confession. At this level, confession opens the door of repression, flooding your inmost self with light and healing: peace, joy, and love. The fear of the Lord is indeed the beginning of authentic living (Ps. 111)!

3
Projection or Repentance?

Fears trigger both projection and repentance. Projection means pretending you have no badness in you and blaming everyone else for the badness you refuse to face in yourself. Repentance means facing your own badness, confessing it, and suffering the pain of changing your ways and growing up. This chapter flows out of the previous one as consequences follow actions. Projection is what happens when repression takes over. Repentance is what happens when confession has its way.

Projection Without Repentance

In the last chapter, we reviewed Saul's inability or unwillingness to own up to the failures in his own life. As a result, he lived with a haunting fear that David was after his crown. He projected on David his own desires and ambitions. Accordingly, his hunting of David was really a hunting down of his own fears. Indeed, it was only the realization that David could have killed Saul but instead only took his spear and water flask that forced Saul to admit that it was he, and not David, who was actually the hunter. Saul had fooled himself into believing that David was after him (1 Sam. 26:21), but the facts were a clear indication that Saul was the victim of his own projections.

If Saul's forced admission could have given birth to genuine confession which would have resulted in a true attitude of re-

pentance and a change of his pattern of living, the story of Saul
may have been quite different. David knew that Saul's admission without repentance was merely a temporary reprieve in
the king's game of intrigue. Accordingly, David abandoned his
homeland for a sojourn in the land of the Philistines (27:1-3).
Only when David was, thus, out of reach did Saul give up his
fear-driven crusade against him (v. 4).

But the flight of David did not solve Saul's fears, it only increased them. He then projected his concerns on the Philistines. Moreover, with the death of Samuel, Saul lost his crystal
ball and his comforting sense of having a pipeline to God. Saul
had been fearful before. After Samuel's death, he became terrified (28:5). He sought desperately for some assurance and
contact with God by all the modes which the people of God
had used previously (v. 6). But the Bible is silent concerning
Saul's humbling of himself before God. When the ancient patterns failed to work for Saul, he turned in utter desperation to
the use of a forbidden witch or medium. Disguising himself,
he consulted the witch of Endor and begged that she would
conjure up Samuel to tell him his fortune (vv. 8-14). What Saul
heard from his seance, however, confirmed his most fearful
projections about himself and about David's future. Saul's terror sapped him of his strength and depleted him of his courage
(v. 20). Thereafter, it was only a matter of time before his army
was defeated and he and his sons lay dead on the battlefield
(31:1-6).

Projection is a cruel slave driver that leads the unwary pilgrim to something like John Bunyan's Slough of Despond. If
you take this way you come to an important fork of the road.
Psychologically the two road signs read: "Punishing Others"
and "Punishing Yourself." Blaming people and events outside
yourself often leads to punishing others for the faults you
sense in yourself but are not willing to face. Blaming yourself
for everything that goes wrong leads to punishing yourself

whether it is really your fault or not. Unhappily both roads end up in the dead end of Dragonwood. If you are blaming yourself for everything, your fears may rob you of the hope of ever getting out of the dark forest. The hopelessness that grows into panic is the theme of the next chapter. Here the spotlight is on blaming others to keep from facing up to your own short-comings or making peace with yourself as an imperfect person.

For the blamer, the next fork in the road forces a choice between projection and repentance. The choice is a hard one. Seeing your own inner ugliness can make you feel horrible. It can prompt a fear of losing control of your life, of becoming weak and subject to cruel punishments. Even worse, you can feel like a nothing, a nobody. You can feel as if you are being driven out of your place in the world into a desert place, alone, deformed, and despised.

Projection Giving Way to Repentance

One of the most fascinating Old Testament personalities, Elijah, illustrates the point. Few people in the holy Scriptures experienced such a sense of touching the unfathomable power of God as the Gilead prophet from Tishbe (1 Kings 17:1). The story of his confrontation with the priests of Baal and his prayer for the fire of God on Mount Carmel is one of the most dramatic moments in Israel's history (18:17-40). When the story is further set within the context of Elijah's role in bringing, by the hand of God, both a severe drought (17:2-7) and then a drenching rain (18:41-46), the sheer sense of power in Elijah's relationship with God is overwhelming.

Yet the powerful prophet was rendered a frustrated, fearful coward by the death threat of Queen Jezebel (19:2-3). He fled for his life from the Northern Kingdom to the remote desert of the South (the Negeb) and pleaded with God that he should die (v. 4). At that point, his entire life seemed to him to be little else than a terrible experience of wilderness. Moreover, his fear of Jezebel led him into the process of projection and scapegoat-ing. The record of his dialogue with God which follows is one of the truly intriguing texts of the Bible.

After God supplied His exhausted escape artist with food, and after the prophet had found a cave for a temporary resi-dence, God asked him what he was doing in the desert. Eli-jah's response is classic. In effect, he said, "I am faithful, but your people are faithless. As a result, I am the only one who is left to honor you and they are trying to kill me" (vv. 9-10).

The conversation is a model of how confused the people of God can become when they are motivated by fear. There was, indeed, some truth to Elijah's concern. The people had not been very faithful and the situation in Israel was bad. But be-yond the truth of these matters, it is essential to recognize that Elijah's fear clouded his perceptions. He failed to realize that he was hardly being obedient himself in fleeing to the South. God brought this fact home to him by repeating the question, "Why are you here?" (vv. 9,13). Given Elijah's perceptions, he probably ought to have said that there was nobody left—*not even me!* Yet Elijah failed to see his own problems and he put the blame on the people of God. He thus divorced himself from the bad situation and used the people as his scapegoat. But God did not let him get away with his attempt at projec-tion. Certainly the people had a problem, but so did their fa-mous prophet. In addition, Elijah's fear did not permit him to recognize reality as it was. He thought he was the only one who was committed to the Lord. God, therefore, had to re-mind His servant that God's special number were still faithful in Israel. They formed a devoted remnant (v. 18). Moreover, if Elijah was going to be part of that remnant, then he himself had better get the message, head back North, and do God's work, too. (vv. 15-16).

Repentance: For the Worldly and the Religious

When things get bad enough for you, when your excuses break down, when you can no longer keep from admitting that some of your troubles are your own fault, you are exposed to the possibility of confession and repentance.

Repentance *(mentanoia)* is one of the great biblical concerns. It is not merely an experience of remorse *(metamelomai)* like the admission by Saul of his guilt. It deals instead with a rejection of the way one is living and a "change of heart." It involves a willingness to accept one's wrongful ways, to own one's guilt, and a readiness to change one's life in accordance with a new perspective. Repentance is a basic ingredient of genuine transformation.

The three parables in Luke 15 form a helpful pictorial description of some important aspects of repentance. The first two stories—the lost sheep and the lost coin—seem on the surface simply to portray the concern of God for those in the helpless state of lostness. But the conclusion of both parables suggests a wider dimension to the stories. Certainly the lost sheep needs a searching shepherd and the lost coin needs a searching housekeeper to bring both of them back into the context of a caring protection. But there is more to those stories than the searchers. The joy of heaven in both of these stories is not merely to be seen as the result of the searcher's work. More important, the sheep and coin are made to represent a straying person who needs repentance (vv. 7,10). These two parables, therefore, serve as a great introduction to one of the truly magnificent stories of the Bible.

Even apart from any consideration of inspiration, the third parable, the prodigal son (or the story of the two sons and the father), is without doubt a world-class story. It catches so much of human experience that almost everyone can echo "I know some people like the ones in that story." The younger son could be the family dreamer who thinks that if he could gain a little freedom from the fearful drudgery of the commonness in everyday life, he would be able to take the world by the tail. The older son, on the other hand, could be one of those resentful, fearful people who has always been the good little person in the family and who, even though hating the commonness of life, thinks that everyone ought to live life the same way.

The manner in which the story is told tends to conform the reader's identification with the younger son rather than the older one. Something deep within us seems to side with the underdog. In such a story, self-righteousness is an attitude we do not accept easily. We hope for wayward kids to find a happy ending to life. So, the British, as far back as Shakespeare, expected a wayward Prince of Wales like Hal, when he came of age and mounted the throne as Henry V, to leave the sins and friends of his youth behind. We do not like waywardness but we find reasons to accept it in youth (as long as it is not an "evil" like murder). Many expect that simply growing up will result in transformation.

But merely growing up is not the message of the lost son. The squandered property was not returned to the younger boy and the pig food was a genuine reflection of his horrible state. When he owned up to his disgusting situation, he recognized that he had actually sinned both against God ("heaven" was a typical Jewish substitute word for God) and his father (v. 18). In his journey back home he was very realistic and did not plead for sonship. All he asked was for servanthood (v. 19). The waiting father accepted him as genuinely repentant and rejoiced like the angels of God when a sinner truly repents (compare vv. 10,22-24).

Now the older son had quite a different feeling about his brother's return and the subsequent party. The older boy had worked hard for his father and had never had a party for himself. He viewed his labor-relationship to his father as that of a servant to a master, and he said so (v. 29). The thought of his father giving a party for his immoral brother was absolutely detestable. It hardly takes much imagination, therefore, to sense what the older boy must have thought. Undoubtedly, he would have projected on his brother thoughts of cheating him out of his inheritance and "taking" the old man for a second time. After all, it was party time in a home that did not have much partying. Would you blame the older son for being suspicious? The property which the father had left was destined to belong to him and this "scum of the earth" brother had returned to upset the situation.

But the father understood the genuine nature of the younger son's repentant heart. He knew his lost son had owned up to the sinfulness of his ways and the pathetic state of his life. Moreover, the father did not need to hear the whole rehearsed confession. He knew the genuineness of the boy's repentance and the father's acceptance was crucial to the boy's transformation. In the Bible new clothing (v. 22) is a symbol of new life, just as transformation is described in Colossians 3:5-14 by the terms "put off" and "put on" as you would clothing.

Yet, while the father accepted the younger boy's repentance, the father was not spineless like the older boy probably projected he would be. The property would belong to the older boy, but that son had a lesson to learn as well. He may not have gone to a far country to show his rejection of his father's accepting spirit, but neither did he evidence the father's sense of love by staying home. The story closes leaving us to wonder whether the older boy chose to continue in his hardness of heart or had a change of heart and accepted the father's spirit of forgiveness. The story closes leaving no doubt, however, that a change of heart is the first step on a spiritual journey for both the worldly and the religious. The waiting father had successfully waited for his younger son. He still had to wait for the elder one.

Two Ways of Being Religious

The two sons embody two ways of being religious. The psychological names for these two ways are extrinsic and intrinsic. The extrinsic way of being religious is not the same as the way of projection, but extrinsic religion makes it easier for a person to slip into the projective way of self-deception and blaming. Intrinsic religion fosters the way of repentance—of being honest with yourself and more concerned about how you look in God's eyes than looking perfect in your own.

Usually the extrinsic and intrinsic ways of being religious are both present in a person. One tends to be the preferred way, however, and thus to control you more than the other. You can shift the balance from one to the other, but change is usually show and painful once your preference is set. Seeing yourself in the light of these two ways of being religious and trusting the way of repentance is a sure way of growing a mature faith.

You may want to use the following[1] description of these two ways to be a yardstick by which to take your own measurement religiously.

INTRINSIC	EXTRINSIC
Strong devotional life. Open to intense religious experience.	Tends to be closed to religious experience.
Guided by inmost Self, understood as Spirit of God.	Guided by expectations of in-group; follows the rules.
Faith is of ultimate significance as a guide to living; gives life meaning.	Faith is superficial; beliefs selectively held. Expedient. Not integrated into daily life.
High self-esteem.	Low or confused self-esteem.
Unselfish, altruistic; holds to brotherhood ideals, love of neighbor as self.	Selfish, self-serving, defensive, protective. Materialistic: money, prestige, and power.

Sees people as unique individuals, more like than unlike oneself. Low prejudice based on race, status, sex, or age.	Sees people in terms of social categories: sex, age, status; more unlike than like oneself. High prejudice based on status, sex, or age.
God is loving and trustworthy at all times, negating powerless feelings and supporting self-esteem.	God is unloving, wrathful, and punishing; impersonal, distant. Evokes feelings of powerlessness and external control.
A low fear of death.	A high fear of death.
High frequency of church attendance.	Low frequency of church attendance.

A curious finding about prejudice comes out of psychological research. Studies that compared religious and nonreligious people on the basis of church membership found that church members were more prejudiced than nonmembers. When the basis of comparison was changed, a surprising difference came to light. Religiously *active* people were compared with religiously *inactive* and also with nonreligious people. Findings then show that religiously *very active* people and nonreligious people are less prejudiced than relatively *inactive* religious people. The casual attender is the most prejudiced of all churchgoers. In social research, designations like active and inactive are fairly easy to quantify, but they may not really be the most helpful for our purposes here. Clearly what these findings suggested to researchers is that religion comes in different forms. The work of Gordon Allport and others on extrinsic and intrinsic types of religion grew out of the hunch that religiosity is not one thing, but many. Attention to prejudice in relation to the intrinsic/extrinsic categories resulted, then, in the findings shown above. Those who have an intrinsic faith are relatively unprejudiced, while their extrinsic neighbors, who make up the majority of churchgoers, show high levels of bigotry. The problem of prejudice boils down, then, not to religion or nonreligion, but to the kind of faith a person has, whether extrinsic or intrinsic.[2]

Two Ways of Being in the World

The ground out of which spring these two ways of being religious is the choice people make between two ways of being in the world—the ways of projection and repentance. One way is to do anything within your power to avoid looking at yourself as you really are. The other way is to risk looking at yourself in the light of the truth about yourself. One way is to blame others for everything that bothers you or goes wrong in the world, in order not to look at yourself. The other way is to turn toward the light about yourself no matter how painful. Projection stops growth; repentance stimulates growth emotionally and spiritually. Projection leads to crimes against life and liveliness. Repentance frees for living abundantly.

An old story tells about a person who took a walk after a rainstorm. At the road's edge, something sparkled in the sun's rays. The traveler bent over to investigate. Unknown to the curious walker, it was a mirror glittering in the mud. After wiping it clean with a sleeve, the person looked into the mirror and said, "My, this is ugly and worthless." So, the traveler tossed it away and continued walking on the way.

The story tells a lot about the "projection" way of being in the world. If your first reaction is to project blame on others it is not necessarily a sign that you are without a conscience. Your conscience may catch your attention, like the mud-smeared mirror in the sun. You are not willing, however, to admit that there could be anything ugly about yourself. Such an admission would feel too painful. So immediately you see the ugliness as something outside of yourself. What you see is ugly, but what you see cannot be inside you. So, you toss it and go on your way.

What you toss aside is the truth about yourself. In not looking at the truth about yourself, you may be tossing aside your child, your spouse, your friend, or neighbor. What you save is your own image of yourself. You keep up appearances—in your own eyes at least.

What others may feel or think about your behavior is of little concern to you. If possible, you do not even let the other people in your life feel anything critical about you. You make them think they are bad to feel critical of you. Usually you have to become a clever talker to convince them that they are the problem while you are entirely above blame.

In family life, a blamer must impose some very strict rules on everyone else in the family. If projection is your way, you most likely have laid down the following great commandments for the family:

Thou shalt not *see* a flaw in me!

Thou shalt not *feel* a critical feeling about me!

Thou shalt not *speak* a critical word against me!

Thou shalt not *believe* anyone except me!

Are you tired of always blaming others? Do you long to be honest with yourself, to relax and take off your suit of armor for a few moments? Can you sense how much energy you are spending in keeping up the image of perfection? Do you sense a growing hardness in your heart? Hardness of heart can be fatal to your inmost self.

Hardness of Heart or a Change of Heart

The hardness of the heart (see Deut. 15:7) and stiffness of the neck (see Neh. 9:16-17) are expressions which biblical writers use to indicate a strong disinterest or lack of concern for other people, especially those in need. It is also used to identify someone who seems firmly committed to the rejection of the ways of God, God's servants, and God's own self. The Pharaoh and the Egyptians during the Exodus period became for the biblical writers a symbol of those who stubbornly take a stand against the purposes of God (see 1 Sam. 6:6). Indeed, the hardening of Pharaoh's heart is not simply attributed to Pharaoh's own decision. The biblical writers considered that God had an active role in confirming Pharaoh's opposition (see Ex. 4:21; 9:12; 11:10; 14:8).

Hardheartedness, then, is often paralleled in the Bible to sinning with the high hand. It is a damnable style of life because it implies doing something knowing that it is contrary to God's will. To be cleansed from sins of the high hand, therefore, required more than sacrifice. It required the personal intervention of God as in the case of David's sin with Bathsheba. Hardness of heart is the opposite of a heart filled with love, kindness, and a sense of understanding. Hardness of the heart places the self at the center of one's universe. It is a companion to the idolatry of the self and it is diametrically opposed to the spirit of repentance.

In the Book of Hebrews the inspired writer, relying on a quotation from Psalm 95:8, called on all Christians to avoid a hard heart (3:8,15; 4:7). He is convinced that hardheartedness makes it impossible to avoid the deceptions of sin (3:13); to be a true participant in Christ (v. 14). Like the Israelites who died in the wilderness (vv. 16-17), those who follow the way of hardheartedness will fail to experience the promised "rest" of God (vv. 11,18-19; 4:3,6). As a solution to this hardness of heart the biblical preacher issues both a call to repentance and a summons to draw near the Divine throne of grace in order to receive God's wonderful mercy (v. 16).

Is someone close to you suffering from hardness of heart? You can help them and help yourself as well. Victims of hardheartedness are, in the words of Scott Peck, "people of the lie."

They are trapped in habits of lying to themselves. They twist the truth and blame people not so much to deceive others as to deceive themselves. The pain of facing ugliness or unworthiness in themselves is so great that they will do anything to be righteous in their own eyes. Projection becomes in time a self-righteous way of life.

Scott Peck sums up his description of people of the lie in these words:

> The problem is not a defect of conscience but the effort to deny the conscience its due. We become evil by attempting to hide from ourselves. The wickedness of the evil is not committed directly, but indirectly as a part of this coverup process. Evil originates not in the absence of guilt but in the effort to escape it.[3]

You can help the self-righteous person in your family or in your friendship circle by not letting yourself be bound by the "Great Commandments" that the blamer tries to impose on you. Give yourself permission to *see* projection for what it is; to *feel* the injustice of being made the butt of another person's faults; and then to *speak* the truth as you know it.

To stand up to people of the lie in this way calls for you to *believe* in yourself as a person created in the image of God. Fortunately you are not called to stand alone. Instead, you allow the image of God in you to rise up and speak the truth. The word of truth not only will make you free but also will offer the possibility of setting the blamer free from the awful burden of pretending a perfection that no human being can honestly claim. Your courage and truth speaking can open a crack in a person's hardened heart that will give God a chance to call the blamer to repentance and to bring about a change of heart.

Courage like this turned Stephen into the first Christian martyr, but it also cracked open the hardened heart of Saul, the great persecutor of the church, enabling God to transform him into the great apostle to the Gentiles. Stephen was a powerful witness. He may not have had the education of Saul/Paul but he surely could detail the failure of the Jews in their relationship with God (Acts 7:2-50). His conclusion was that for all their righteous talk, the Jews were really a hardhearted, stiff-necked people who refused to listen to God's spokesmen. They not only persecuted the prophets but killed God's personal representative on earth (vv. 51-53). This historical lecture by Stephen was undoubtedly a necessary corrective to a starry-eyed view of Jewish history. But the persecutors were outraged by what came next. The condemned Stephen told them that, while he spoke, he saw a vision of God with the living Jesus at God's right hand (vv. 55-56). Moreover, he did not die in anger at his persecutors but modeled for his killers a forgiving spirit like that of Jesus Himself (v. 60; compare Luke 23:34).

Saul and the Jews feared that the Christians would destroy the Jewish faith and they treated them like criminals. The Christians, however, modeled for their Jewish persecutors the fearlessness of truth that makes one free to love and to be kind to the perpetrators of injustice. Can you imagine the impact that the death of Stephen had upon Saul, when on the road to Damascus, he heard the words, "I am Jesus, whom you are persecuting" (Acts 9:5)?

Saul's conversion is an inspiration to everyone, no matter how hard the heart may be. Transformation is possible because God is the author of the changed heart. We humans do not need to continue in a pattern of the hardness of heart. There are two ways of being in the world which are open to everyone: projection and repentance. Projection, which is born in the refusal to face reality honestly, can be transformed by the action of authentic repentance. You, too, can be a vital part of such a change of heart by facing your reality and by speaking the truth to yourself and others in the spirit of love, no matter how upsetting and dangerous that may be for you.

4
Hopelessness or Hope?

In the previous chapter you were asked to step back into your childhood and stand at the fork in the road where you chose your preferred way to cope with life's troubles—either to punish others or to punish yourself. One is the way of blaming others for the faults you sense in yourself but are not willing to face. The other is the way of blaming yourself whether it is really your fault or not. Blaming others, as a way of life, blocks repentance. It causes your soul to shrivel up beneath a mask of respectability. Constantly blaming yourself for everything that goes wrong around you is a symptom of a dangerous spiritual virus. It turns you into a fear-ridden person, making you sick with despair and hopelessness. Hopelessness may turn into panic or fade away into apathy. In any case, hopelessness is a symptom of a very sick soul.

Cut Off from Your Roots

At Christmastime one year a wise, old person stood holding the hand of a child admiring the family Christmas tree. After a long silence, the old one said to the child, "See that tree all full of sap and its needles all green and fresh? It does not know it has been separated from its source. But it will learn. It will learn."

Who has not learned what Christmas trees learn? When the gifts have been opened, the lights unplugged, and the trimmings packed away, when half-bare branches droop and the needles cover the floor, the Christmas tree knows it has been separated from its source. And so do the children who drag the tree away. At some level of awareness everyone knows that rootedness is essential to hope—to remaining green and fresh in spirit.

The Bible is filled with examples of what it means to experience being cut off from your roots. Not only did King Saul experience the reality of being cut off, but another intriguing illustration is the story of Samson, the biblical Achilles or Hercules. In a tragic time when Israel did evil and forsook its God, the messenger of God appeared to Manoah's wife and informed her that she would give birth to a mighty deliverer. But the angel warned her that her son would have to avoid alcohol, unclean foods, and the razor on his hair in the manner of Israel's purity or Nazarite vows (Judg. 13:2-7).

During his lifetime, Samson was blessed and empowered by God (see vv. 24-25; 15:14) but he was attracted by the beauty of Philistine women (14:2), including prostitutes (16:1). These women became for Samson his Achilles heel. He finally succumbed to his weakness by disclosing to the wily Delilah the secret of his God-given strength (vv. 15-17). After she shaved his head while he slept, he thought he could rise and shake off the Philistine threat as he had done previously. But he did not realize that, with his hair gone, divine power had departed from him. He was as weak as any ordinary person (vv. 17,20).

Thus, Samson was separated from the source of his strength, like the Christmas tree of an earlier illustration. He had lived his life in such a way that the worldly woodman's axe divided the tree from its roots. Reality then set in very quickly as he was forced to live out the rest of his life blind and imprisoned. Never again was he free from the signs of his cut-off state.

Samson became like the leafy barren fig tree of Mark 11:12-14,20-21 which promised to be productive but was empty of fruit. Jesus' curse upon the tree continues to remind us that externals are not the test of a genuine reality, whether it pertains to people or to institutions. Between the two parts of the barren fig tree story Mark has placed the account of the cleansing of the Temple (vv. 15-19). By organizing the story in this way, Mark wanted his readers to understand very clearly that internal deadness can apply to a God-given institution like the Temple, or a congregation, or a Sunday School class, just as much as to a seemingly God-inspired person. As such, it is a warning to all of us not to take our rootedness for granted. Our task is to seek for the true source of rootedness and hope in this world.

Rootedness Is Essential

Rootedness in the life of the Spirit is essential. It is like a child in the arms of a caring grandparent. The child receives quiet joy and confidence for growing up. It is like a young woman or man who is chosen by the adult whom they most admire to join in an important task. They feel a leaping of the heart in joy, a surging of a deeply rooted inner strength, a current of hope for the future.

When you experience the Presence of God as an inner voice saying, "Fear Not! For I am with you," you discover the true rootedness of the soul. Rooted and grounded in the Presence of God, you can face anything. You know the truth of Viktor Frankl's words, as he reflected on his years in a Nazi concentration camp: a person who has a "why" for living can endure any "how" of living. Being rooted in the experience of God's Presence, your soul blossoms with hope. You have the "why" for living. The Presence of God awakens a joy that the world cannot give. It is the hope that sustains you even in the valley of the shadow of death.

Paul's Example to the Philippians

Among the great messages of joy and hope in the New Testament stands the Letter to the Philippians. It is a magnificent mirror which reveals some incredible aspects of the heart of

Paul. As he wrote this epistle, Paul was under constant guard in a Roman prison (1:13). He was beset by criticism from rival preachers and teachers of the gospel (v. 15; 3:2-3). And he was greatly concerned for the health and well-being of his few nearby, supporting friends like Epaphroditus (2:25-30). It is difficult to conceive of a human situation in which one could find more reason for feeling uprooted and cut off from hope. Yet the advice Paul gave to his Macedonian friends sounds like it must be coming from someone who was experiencing just the opposite situation.

He opened with a joyful prayer for his readers (1:4) and with a sense of confidence that God would bring to fulfillment the divine work in them so that they would experience the great day of the coming of Christ (vv. 6-11). While he missed them very much (v. 8), he told them he was convinced that God was able to use his imprisonment to bring the gospel to the Roman guard and to give courage in witnessing to other Christians who knew about his boldness for Christ (vv. 12-14). He did not castigate his critics but he praised God for the fact that the gospel was going out, even if it was being spread for the wrong personal reasons (vv. 15-18).

When you read words like these, does it not almost seem as though you are experiencing a dream? Can anybody really be that unselfish? Oh, we all know some Christians who use nice words to hit other people over the head. But how many people do you know that in their very essence are as self-giving as Paul? How many do you know who accept a criticism of their Christianity and praise God that through everything Christ is being proclaimed? How many churches do you know that are more concerned about the unselfish proclamation of the gospel than about gathering sheep? What about you? How do you measure up to this Paul who was facing the possibility that the emperor might very soon cut off his existence?

Paul took seriously the possibility of his approaching death.

And from his pen came the classic words, "For to me to live is Christ, and to die is gain" (v. 21). Perhaps you noticed, that in the Bible there seem to be two concepts of being "cut off." Death in this world is something that everyone experiences. But there is also a realm that the Christian knows which is far more significant than life in this world. It is the realm of one's life and relationship with God. To be cut from the roots of life in this world is one matter, but to be separated from life with God is a matter of far greater significance.

The Book of Philippians is the exciting testimony of Paul that when one is rooted properly in God, the tragic experiences that normally uproot people can become pathways to a greater sense of meaning and hope. No one of us prays for tragedy. But the genuine Christian strives to understand the model of the self-giving Christ who became obedient to death (2:5-8). In that pilgrimage the Christian glimpses some of the amazing truth in Paul's thesis that God has bestowed upon us the privilege not only to believe but also to suffer for Christ's sake (1:29). To be a follower of Jesus and a servant like Paul means to deliver to Christ the fears of being human and to accept willingly the model of the suffering and the dying Jesus which overcomes fear. It is to be able to say with Paul, "Rejoice in the Lord. . . . Let everyone know your self-giving patience. . . . The Lord is near. . . . Do not be anxious about anything. . . . Let your concerns be known to God. . . . The peace of God . . . will guard your hearts and your minds in Christ Jesus" (4:4-7). These are the words of one who has truly discovered the secret of rootedness and hope.

Two Ways of Being Rooted

Hope is often confused with mere excitement. When hope is nothing more than excitement about some new thing to do or to have, it is a hope that is separated from its source. It is not the hope that is rooted and grounded in the union of your inmost self with the Spirit of God. These two levels of hope point up two ways of being rooted.

In the conclusion to the Sermon on the Mount (Matt. 7:24-27), Jesus illustrated these two ways of being rooted with a parable of two different houses. People who are responsive to God's will in their lives are like a house whose foundation is built on solid rock and in spite of torrents of rain and destructive wind that house will stand firm. But other people who hear God's Word and fail to put it into practice are like a house that is built on shifting sand. When the storms hit such a house, the footings give way and the house collapses because there is no foundation that holds it together.

The comparison of the two houses has a wonderful counterpart picture in James 1:22-25. In that text those who hear the Word of God and do not gain the stability that comes from a life of practicing their faith are likened to persons who look into a mirror and, when turning away, they promptly forget in whose image they are formed or what they look like. Those who are properly founded, however, know the image they represent; and they persevere in the image of their God, even when they are not in worship service, reading the Bible, or praying with other Christians.

The stability of the properly imaged person and the foundation of the correctly constructed house are universal pictures which do not lose their meaning even in a space-age society. The biblical writers were captivated by the idea of having the correct foundation or basis for stability. Indeed, in the Book of Revelation the symbols of sand and rock are used again to portray the fact that the two ways of being rooted have superhuman powers behind each picture. In Revelation 12:17 (or 13:1) the dragon, the enemy of Jesus, is pictured in some translations (see for example the RSV) as standing on the shifting sands of the sea whereas Jesus, the Lamb, and His servants are standing on the solid foundation of Mount Zion (Rev. 14:1).

Gaining a personal sense of stability, like constructing a new home on a solid foundation, is a crucial matter. Many have found great excitement in building a new house. It awakens hope of happiness in personal well-being and joy in family living. If the foundation is not right, however, the new house may offer more grief than joy. High hopes quickly turn into despair. These two ways of being rooted and grounded make all the difference in keeping fears from filling the new house and turning hope into hopelessness.

Here is how the theme of a solid foundation can be lived out in the life of a person today.

The Traditional Way of Being Rooted

I shall call her Viola.[1] Viola grew up in a family that lived a quiet and orderly life of work, church attendance, and family friends. At age sixty she was admitted to a psychiatric hospital with a church phobia. At first she withdrew from the front pews where her family customarily sat. Then she used the pews closest to the door. Finally she was not able to attend church at all. Neither could she go out to restaurants or other public places. She began to feel that people were closing in on her, that she was being suffocated, even in her own house. The more she tried to resist these terrible feelings, the more she was overcome with panic. Fear finally possessed her completely.

As you read Viola's life story, you may wish to keep in mind the parable of the two houses and ask yourself why her foundation was not solid enough to survive the first real storm that hit her.

Viola's father was kind, heavyset, quiet, warm, soft-spoken, very hardworking, not inclined to show affection physically though he was quite capable of feeling it. Her mother was heavyset, hardworking and strict to the point of making her children afraid to speak up or express their feelings. She, too, did not show much affection physically, but her children never doubted that she loved them in her way.

In growing up, nobody close to Viola died, had a serious

illness, or suffered any major injury. She remembered nothing
about her own emotional life in growing up except to describe
herself as "a happy child, a little shy." She joined the church at
age seven, feeling that she was getting "closer to God."

In her middle teens, Viola was "dying to go to work" because she wanted to dress like "a young lady." She wanted a
pair of high-heeled shoes most of all, but her parents opposed
it. She lied to her mother and got a job, but when her father
found out she had lied, he slapped her. She kept the job, however, bought the shoes, and felt great satisfaction. "At home
we were happy," she said. "We had everything we wanted. My
parents gave us clothes. Whatever we wanted, we had it
there."

At eighteen she married. Her mother invited the son of family friends to dinner. He was twenty-four and already owner of
his own business. Viola was not told he was coming to dinner,
but when she met him, she liked him. "It was mutual love at
first sight," she reported. A year and a half later she had a baby
boy. Five years later she gave birth to a girl. Both events were
described as "a very good experience."

No major events took place until Viola was thirty-eight. Her
father died within three days of a stroke. She did not cry, but
looked at him in the coffin as though "he was sleeping" and
resented that "they were taking him away from us." Two years
later her mother died. Viola's only reported response was to
say that she was sad. The next year her son got married, however, and Viola was devastated. She felt "empty" and could not
eat for three days and remained "very sad for a long time" because, as she said, "I was not prepared to let him go." She was
more prepared for her daughter's marriage six years later, comforting herself in the realization that her daughter would live
nearby.

Soon after the daughter's wedding, however, Viola's husband had a renal colic in the night. Viola felt he was dying. It

was a terrifying night for her. She was fifty years old at the time. Immediately after this Viola developed the first signs of her church phobia and high blood pressure. Ten years later she was admitted to the psychiatric hospital.

As soon as she was admitted to the psychiatric hospital her symptoms disappeared completely. She was unable, however, to deal with any negative emotions or thoughts, especially anger toward those whom she loved. She was embarrassed as she recognized her anger and covered it up with expressions of love and affection. It soon became obvious to her doctor that she was determined not to inform herself about the sources of her anxiety and phobia. She wanted relief without knowledge of the underlying feelings that had overpowered her. She did not want to take responsibility to free herself from being the victim of her own feelings.

Gradually some of her phobic reactions diminished. Several factors helped: her therapist's listening to her fears; the support of her husband and children; her wakening to the significance of being a grandmother, and realizing that she could live for her several grandchildren. Viola regained some hope for living. She lost her claustrophobia about public places and her own home, but her church phobia continued to plague her.

The resistance of her church phobia to healing is of special interest here. While she was in the hospital, Viola was asked many questions about her religious experiences and her thoughts and feelings about God. A careful analysis revealed that her feelings about God were almost identical to her feelings about her human father. In talking about her life, Viola listed her father as the most loved person from age six to the day of her father's death. She then said, "My father died. I always felt closer to my father. Then I changed from him to my husband and children."

Viola was asked to draw a picture of God. She had described father as a "mustachioed man," and when she talked about the picture she had drawn of a clean-shaven God, she commented with embarrassment, "I didn't even put whiskers on him."

In many ways Viola unveiled a private god who was a domestic divinity. Her god had none of the transcendent qualities that characterize the God of organized religion. Viola's god had only the traits that fit her wishes for protection and harmony. Her god fitted the needs of preadolescent children but was much too small for adult living.

In summary, Viola is an example of a woman who never had enough frustration in growing up to question the adequacy of her childhood god. Instead she reduced the whole cosmos to the size of her own household. She could not imagine it any other way. In her household, then, god was one more domestic fixture.

It was only when life threatened to take away her husband and her children—her real God substitutes—that she collapsed. Had she been able to admit her anger against God, she might have discovered that hers was only a little household deity. Unable to risk seeing the true God above the household gods, Viola was stripped of outside help to cope with the hard blows of life. She reacted with anxiety and phobias. She was overcome by fear as if it were the face of evil. Had she learned to fear the God of gods she would have been at the "beginning of wisdom" and so been prepared to hear the Divine word of assurance: "Fear Not!"

Viola was rooted indeed. But she was rooted in her family of origin and in a tradition that protected girls from the pain of growing up and becoming mature persons in their own right. She was handed from her father to her husband in the ritual of marriage, but she did not "leave" her father's house for her husband's until after her father's death. In a sense she did not ever find her own house. All her life she avoided meeting her own inmost self. Viola was a good church member, but she never knew what it meant to "seek first the kingdom of God." She did not understand what Jesus was saying in His warning that a person who loves father or mother "more than me is not worthy of me," and one who "loves son or daughter more than me is not worthy of me," and one "who does not take [the] cross and follow me is not worthy of me." Viola "found" her life in her family tradition—and she "lost" it at age fifty. She may never have allowed herself even to look at the promise that follows these warnings: that the person who loses her life for my sake "will find it" (Matt. 10:37-39).

Another Way of Being Rooted: Pilgrimage

Where and how do you find your life if not in being enmeshed in a family tradition and being a blind believer in the ways of your church? The biblical way is to risk life as a pilgrimage. A pilgrim is one who leaves home. In leaving home, a pilgrim takes the risks of getting stuck in questions without finding the answers. On pilgrimage you are in danger of terrorists, of detours, and of losing your direction. Pilgrims, like Moses and the Israelites of old, wandered in the wilderness for forty years before they were able to find the way into the Promised Land.

Yet there is something more to pilgrimage: "Promised Land" is the clue! A pilgrimage is a journey that goes somewhere. A pilgrim is not a tourist who spends time merely sightseeing and whose goal is to return to the place of beginning. A pilgrim's journey is from the house of birthing and rearing to the soul's true home. A pilgrim cuts the old roots with the City of Earth. Pilgrims are rooted in the City of God toward which they journey. Pilgrimage is a journey of the soul toward the Promised Land of becoming godlike in love.

The Bible's leading model of the pilgrim person is Abraham, the father of Israel's faith. In the call of the Mesopotamian Abram from Haran, God set about to teach the world that

God was not merely a settled God whose actions were limited to a piece of land. The divine goal was to make a pilgrim people and through that people to bless the entire world (Gen. 12:2).

The life of Abram, like the life of most pilgrims, was not an easy one. He received the promise at Bethel after traveling many miles. The promise was that the land upon which he was standing would someday become the home of his descendants (v. 7). But Abram was not able to settle there. His pilgrimage continued because of drought and famine in the land. So he journeyed to Egypt where food was still available (v. 10). After a less than honorable attempt at saving his skin by deceiving the Pharaoh (vv. 11-20), however, he returned to the Negeb in Palestine where his servants and those of his nephew (Lot) fought over land rights for feeding their sheep (13:1-7). In the settlement of this dispute Abram showed a superb quality to his life by allowing Lot, his junior partner, to claim the most fertile land for grazing (vv. 8-13). Nevertheless, God knew the heart of this servant Abram and God confirmed to the servant the promise that all of the properties he saw from that point would someday fall to his descendants (vv. 14-18).

Yet the big question was: How could Abram's descendants inherit the land when Abram had no children? So, as he beheld the sky with its innumerable stars, God announced that Abram's children would be numberless. Then the biblical narrator says that Abram believed God and it was accounted to him as righteousness (15:6). But still Abram had no children! So by a neat little scheme Abram and Sarai tried to help God fulfill the promise of a child through the slave woman Hagar (16:1-15). But that plot was not God's way of dealing with the promise to Abram. Instead, God reaffirmed the covenant, changed Abram's name to Abraham (father of a multitude), instructed him to begin the rite of circumcision as a sign of the covenant, and promised a son to his renamed wife, Sarah

(17:1-16). The birth of Isaac accordingly became the thrilling answer to God's promise (21:1-7).

That birth, however, had a dark side as well. Only one son was to be the son of promise and the rivalry which Abraham and Sarah created by the scheming birth of Ishmael led to a hard experience of separation for Abraham (vv. 8-21). Moreover, God had a test that would surely clarify the genuineness of Abraham's faith. That test, recorded in Genesis 22, is one of the great stories of the Bible. The near sacrifice of Isaac proved for all generations of Bible readers that when Abraham was tested he proved beyond a shadow of a doubt that obedience to God was truly the primary commitment of his life.

This pilgrim father of Israel thus became the symbol for all God's people of what it means to live in faith with a sense of expectant hope. From his life story it is quite clear that Abram/Abraham was not totally consistent in his dependence upon God. But it is absolutely clear that his commitment to God, ultimately far outweighed his personal quest. When, therefore, the time came for him to be counted as obedient to God, he proved himself to be a man of faithful commitment.

Thus, Abraham become the model in the New Testament of what it means to be a person of faith. While Martin Luther had great difficulty perceiving the unity of the message of faith in the Books of Romans and James, it is absolutely certain that Paul and James had little difficulty agreeing that Abraham was the choice model of a person of faith (see Rom. 4:1-24; Jas. 2:18-24). Moreover, in the roll call of the faithful in the Book of Hebrews, Abraham is portrayed as the central symbol of faith (Heb. 11:8-19). He clearly stands as the pilgrim model who sought for the city of God. He is pictured as having believed God in spite of the logic of sacrifice. The great preacher of Hebrews argued that even if God had to bring back Isaac from the dead, Abraham was willing to trust that God's promises through Isaac would be fulfilled.

According to the Bible, therefore, pilgrimage is a life of trusting God even when the situation seems hopeless. It is the way of dealing with the monsters of fear by risking one's commitment upon the God who can see beyond the terror-producing situations of life. It is a willingness to go with Jesus outside the protection of the ancient camp where the terrors of wilderness confront us (Heb. 13:13). But we go in the confidence that beyond the wilderness is the city of our God (v. 14)!

5
Isolation as a Loner or the Companionship of a Guide

The Swamp of Loneliness

Loneliness is a swamp for the soul. If you were left alone in the swamp long enough as a child, you may well have grown up as a loner. Growing up lonely you would know the fears of a snake-infested swamp. Strange sensations would agitate your body. Bizarre fantasies might grip your mind. Noisy internal voices could browbeat your will to keep you from breaking out of the isolation in which you find yourself. In such a pattern your private space would be a safe harbor in which you could escape from the turbulence and dangers of the people world. But it would also be a prison cell.

You can live alone without being a loner. And not all loners live alone. Your isolation as a loner is more an internal matter than an external one. Some loners wear pleasant masks of sociability. Others advertise by their appearance, posture, and behaviors that they wish to be left alone. What loners have in common is fear and pain—fear and pain inflicted very early in life, unchecked, and unrelieved. It is the fear and pain of weakness, compounded by feeling unloved and unlovable.

The plight of a loner is like that of a person who is thrown overboard into the sea as a child with only a life jacket. The child survives in spite of the unspeakable terrors of exposure, abandonment, and the chill of death. Once on dry land again, the victim walks around for a long, long time with the life jacket tightly attached.

If you are thrown into life without warm, dependable, and nourishing relationships, you mobilize all your energies to survive. Your real, genuine self gets locked away while you thrash around in search of a safe place that offers some freedom from pain. You long to be born over again, or at least to be awakened to life in relationships that help you grow. You long to see yourself mirrored in someone's eyes—someone who looks on you with delight. You hunger for friends with whom you do not need to be in constant dread of the day they become disgusted with you and walk away.

No wonder then, if you have endured such a condition, that you cling desperately to your life jacket, to your isolation as a loner. It is your only known means of survival—the life jacket which consists of the expectations, demands, and duties you impose on yourself in order to get your daily dole of approval. You develop a false self in the struggle for survival. You wear the mask of a totally self-sufficient person—cool, aloof, self-reliant, strong, and sometimes self-sacrificing. Inwardly, you are afraid, living deep in the swamp of loneliness. You are especially afraid of the night. During the day you walk around on the dry land of adulthood still wearing your life jacket. You try not to notice how hot and heavy it is; how awkward and complicated it makes your life; how odd it makes you look to others; how it closes you off from your true self and from spontaneous enjoyment of others.

Before things can change for the better, however, you will have to find a swimming teacher. Together the two of you will plunge again into the sea of your early fears. Not until you have learned to swim can you feel safe in the sea. Then, with your teacher and friend alongside, you may dare to strip off the life jacket and swim freely to shore. Then, at last you will walk freely on the earth—intimate with yourself, at peace with the tragic story of your childhood, reconciled to what has been and always will be. Finally, you are able to be relaxed and open to others, alive and growing again, and able to hear the voice of the Spirit coming to you with the longed-for words: "Fear not!"[1]

God's Dealing with a Fearful Loner

One of the truly inspiring segments of the Bible involves a young man by the name of Gideon. The story of Gideon is a vivid example of how one can learn to swim in an ocean of fear and loneliness. The story opens in Judges 6 as the country of Israel was in a fearful state of siege. The land was being raped and wasted by the plundering of the Midianites. Moreover, their animals swarmed over the fields and literally denuded the landscape of its vegetation (v. 5). The people of Israel were forced to find shelter in caverns and caves as they fled before the onslaught of the Midianite nomads (v. 2). In their pathetic state the Israelites cried to God, but God's prophet sternly informed them that their sad condition was directly tied to their practical abandonment of God's ways (vv. 1,7-10).

Yet God had a plan for their rescue and it involved a terrified young man, Gideon. As the messenger (angel) of the Lord approached, he addressed Gideon with the greeting, "The Lord is with you, Oh mighty man of valor!" (v. 12). The way the biblical writer portrayed Gideon as alone and hiding at a winepress where he was grinding some wheat so that he would not be discovered by the invaders makes the angel's words seem almost laughable. Who would watch a winepress out of season? It was a perfect place for a fear-stricken young man who was trying to produce a little food, both to work and to hide.

Indeed, the dialogue between Gideon and the angel pretty much confirms the irony in the messenger's words concerning Gideon's strength. He really was feeling hopeless and afraid. Gideon first answered the angel's greeting by taking issue with the messenger's assumption that God was with Israel. It seemed to Gideon that, rather than blessing God's people with

His presence, God had abandoned them (v. 13). Instead of getting into a theological argument, however, God's messenger
simply told Gideon to go and rescue Israel. That message was a
commission from God (v. 14). Gideon's response amounted to
both a question of how such a deliverance was possible and an
excuse that his and his family's resources were the weakest of
anyone in Israel. It was like Moses' excuse that he did not have
the speaking ability to approach Pharaoh (Ex. 4:10). But the
angel's reply to Gideon, a virtual repetition of his greeting,
was "I will be with you" and by your unifying of Israel you
will deliver a knock-out punch to the Midianites (Judg. 6:16).

How do you argue with an angel if you are a mere human
like Gideon? Well, you could ask for a sign to see if this messenger was all that he claimed to be. And that was exactly what
Gideon did (v. 17). But as soon as he did so, he must have realized how dangerous it was not to treat him correctly and make
an appropriate offering to him. So Gideon begged for time and
immediately prepared an offering. When it was all ready, the
angel merely touched the offering with the tip of his rod and
the entire offering exploded into flame (vv. 18-21).

As the fire ate up the offering and the angel disappeared
before his eyes, Gideon was terrified. He realized that he was
in the actual presence of God. That experience meant that he
was as good as dead unless God would grant him peace (shalom)! God did just that.

Can you imagine how Gideon felt when he went home that
night? He was probably exhausted and fell asleep at once. But
you guessed it. The Lord woke him out of his sleep and told
him to tear down the worship centers of the false gods, then
build an altar to Yahweh and sacrifice a bull (the symbol of
Baal) on the new altar. Did he go and do it the next morning?
Not quite. He waited for the dark of night because he was
afraid. Moreover, he got his friends to help him because there
is generally strength in numbers. But what is done at night is

usually visible in the daylight. When the townspeople saw the destruction of the worship centers of their false gods, they discovered who did it; and they were ready to kill Gideon. But thank God for smart fathers. His father suggested that the people let their god Baal kill Gideon, if he was that strong. The people agreed and Gideon felt relieved. Indeed, he began to think that maybe God really had a place for him in the conflict (vv. 25-32).

Accordingly, he sent out a summons to the nearby tribes of Israel to assemble for battle because God was with them. To his surprise, 32,000 Israelites gathered to support his call. But fearful Gideon was still not quite sure God wanted him to take on the Midianite scourge. After all, the Midianites had gathered at least 120,000 (8:10). So Gideon arranged to test God with a sheep fleece. God responded. But that test still did not convince Gideon. So he tried a reverse test and God responded again. Well, those tests convinced Gideon that he ought to be ready for battle (6:36 to 7:1).

But God was not quite ready with Gideon. The Lord had some tests of His own. The odds were four to one. Gideon knew he was outnumbered but that situation was not strange. The Israelites had won with God when they had been outnumbered before. By the time God was finished with His tests, however, Gideon was left with a mere 300 men and the odds were worse than one to four hundred (7:2-7). Do you think Gideon and his little band were afraid at that point? Read Judges 7:9-10. God obviously had some confidence building to do. So He told Gideon to sneak down into the camp of the Midianites with his faithful servant Purah and merely listen to the conversation around the campfire. When Gideon heard the conversation, he could do nothing else than worship God and ready himself for God's miracle.

The story of Gideon is one of the great stories in the Bible of how God can become the swimming instructor to a weak and fearful human being who is terrified by the dreadful ocean of human circumstance. To be a servant of God is not a comfortable way of life. It often means leaving the protection of what we have come to regard as the tolerable, even though fearful, situations of life. It means hearing God's "Fear not," facing the realities of life's situations, and discovering with God that there is liberty waiting beyond the bondage of loneliness and fear.

God's Intention Is Companionship

God's "Fear not" is good news because God's intention is companionship. When the Lord addressed his words of peace to Gideon he really wanted Gideon to learn something about the nature of the Divine presence. God's presence is meant to banish fear and loneliness from the hearts of human beings. Moreover, it is the presence of God among His people that creates the sense of community or family among the people of God. In the Exodus, the pillar of smoke by day and the pillar of fire by night (Ex. 13:17-22) were meant to give the fleeing and terrified Israelites a sense of security and community with their God in spite of the circumstances of their lonely wilderness setting.

It is hard for human beings to learn to sense the calming reality of the divine presence in the midst of fear and turmoil. The disciples could not understand how Jesus was able to sleep in the boat when the waves were swirling about them. Somehow He was not terrified by external circumstances. But they felt lonely and powerless (Mark 4:35-38). They had the difficult lesson to learn about how outside circumstances usually dominate our perception of reality and make us feel empty and alone.

This phenomenon was not an isolated event with the disciples. It is mentioned a number of times as the Gospels give us witness. For example, in John 11, when Lazarus died, all the disciples could think about was the hostility they would confront in Judea. They did not think about the presence of Jesus. They could only think about their enemies in Jerusalem. They preferred to stay in the calm setting of Galilee. Thomas voiced for them their view of Jerusalem and southern Palestine when he said that to go there would mean to die (v. 16). They did not really understand the difference between walking in the darkness and living in the presence of God's light (vv. 9-10). Hopefully, today we can learn from their lack of understanding.

As events in the life of Jesus marched steadily to the crucifixion, John provided his readers with an insight into the farewell instructions of Jesus. Some of these instructions in John 13 to 17 are extremely important for you in your times of loneliness. Jesus knew His disciples would be worried and would feel abandoned when He would leave them. Therefore, in John 14 He focused on their sense of emptiness.

As indicated in Borchert's book, *Assurance and Warning,* the disciples had little sense of peace when Jesus began to talk about his departure.[2] Even though he spoke about preparing a place for them, they had no idea where he was going or how to get there. Thomas, on behalf of the disciples, begged for a road map (John 14:5). Jesus' reply to them—that He was the road map to the Father—hardly satisfied them. Accordingly, Philip, in desperation, asked for just a glimpse of the Father to calm their troubled hearts. Scarcely did he realize what he was requesting because to see God was tantamount to dying, since no one had ever seen God except the Son whose task it was to make Him known (vv. 9-11; see John 1:18).

But Jesus understood what they needed. They needed a companion for life, and therefore He spoke to them of the Holy Spirit (the Paraclete), their new Companion, their new Counselor, Comforter, Advocate, and Supporter. Jesus was not about to abandon them to their own resources. He would not orphan them (v. 18). Instead, He would give them the Holy

Spirit that would provide them with a sense of peace (shalom) in this world and calm their troubled hearts (vv. 26-27). They needed to realize, however, that it was necessary for Jesus to die and leave them in order for the Paraclete to come to them (16:7). After the resurrection the Spirit would be their guide and would teach them concerning the glory of Jesus and about their task on earth (vv. 11-15). But while they were in the state of shock that comes with a sense of loss, they could hardly make sense out of His promises (v. 12).

The day would come after the crucifixion when they would discover a new abiding joy like the joy that comes to a mother after she has experienced the pains of labor and has given birth to a child (vv. 20-22). In that day they would realize a new sense of God's presence in their lives, and they would experience a new power in prayer (vv. 23-24). In that day they would find the answer to loneliness in the companionship of God's Spirit. In that day they would indeed discover the foundation of a new community which is built on a common experience of the power and presence of God in the life of God's people.

Christians, then, are people who have learned what it means to be accepted and adopted by God and who accept one another as children (sons and daughters) of God in Christ Jesus their Lord. They have discovered the oneness in Christ that comes from being loved and accepted by God (17:21). They have experienced the new birth by the Spirit (3:3-7) and have become part of the family of God.

Your Guide Is Ready When You Are

Many a person hears the good news of God's intention toward people as just: "Promises! Promises! Promises!" The guidance of the Holy Spirit may be good enough for those who are not swamp people, but, you may say, "I need a guide I can see, and hear, and touch!" And so you may.

Spiritual masters through the centuries have told their disciples: "When you are ready, your guide will appear." If this is true, the first question is not "Where is my guide?" but "How do I get ready for my guide to appear?" If God accepts you as you are, your guides will come in forms you are able to see and in ways you may receive with a minimum of danger. Your first step, then, may be to imagine yourself trusting the guide who is already standing by waiting for you. As you try to imagine such a thing, try looking for the sacred in the everyday. Seeing the sacred is not some big-deal experience reserved for the privileged few. The sacred is in the everyday stuff of life. You may say, "But I dare not open myself to anyone else. I have been hurt too often, and it is too much to risk it again. I am just plain suspicious of this kind of talk." Know that you do not have to eliminate your suspiciousness. All you need to do is make a slight shift in your suspicions. Try questioning the reliability of the glasses you have worn all your life—with their lenses of fear and pain. For just a moment allow yourself to take off the old glasses and look at the world with newborn eyes.

Your first guide may not be a person at all. One of the places to look for the sacred is in nature. The American artist, Andrew Wyeth, sees the sacred in things. With palette and brush, Wyeth gives them wings. Sometimes a person needs to do nothing more unusual than to locate the print of a painting by an artist who sees the sacred in things, to frame and place it where it can become the focus of daily attention. The artist, then, becomes your guide to seeing the sacred in the stones. Your fear tells you that people will inflict pain. But a person's work of art may be safe enough for you to contemplate until you see within it: "The glory of the One Who moves all things penetrates all the universe and shines in one part more and in another less."[3]

Heartbreak happens, as you know all too well. You move out—beyond nature to people. You begin to trust friendship a little, and then the inevitable happens. You feel abandoned and betrayed like the person in Dragonwood. The old fears return with a vengeance. Only this time try distrusting your fears. Remember that sometimes a trust betrayed is the very thing that opens your eyes to see the sacred inside yourself.

A student once asked the teacher: "I have a question about Deuteronomy 6 which says, 'And these words, which I command you this day, shall be upon your heart.' Why is it said this way? Why are we not told to place them *in* our hearts?"

The teacher replied: "It is not within the power of human beings to place the divine teachings directly in their hearts. All we can do is place them *on* the surface of the heart so that when the heart breaks they drop in."

The teacher's word calls for hope that somehow the Word of God will drop into your broken heart rather than the evil words of self-pity, bitterness, and revenge.

The best hope for all who live in loneliness is to risk another step—in faith. The next step is to move toward the person who seems most likely to be able to recognize the sacred within you, that is, someone who respects you for yourself and may be able to accept you with all your fears and pain. Keep your eyes open to see the difference between people. Some need to use you to meet their own needs. There are others, however, whose basic needs are being met well in their private world; and they may be able to walk with you on your journey, for part of the way at least.

The old fear response will generally kick up again when somebody reaches out to you in a loving way. You will usually try either to withdraw or to attack, hoping to drive such a guide away. Once again, a strong dose of distrust of your old fear reactions may help. And a search for a different way to respond helps, too.

An Insight from Piglet

In a conversation between Winnie-the-Pooh and his little friend, Piglet, you may sense just such an option. Try to imagine yourself as Piglet—little and very fearful, but longing for the courage to accept a friend's gift of care.

Pooh has just written a song called "Tiddely-Pom." Pooh sang all seven stanzas for Piglet; and, when Pooh finished, Piglet could not say a word. He just stood and glowed. No one had ever sung "Ho" for Piglet before—"Ho" all for himself!

Had Piglet been able to say what he really felt, he would have asked for one of the stanzas over again. It was the stanza beginning "O gallant Piglet," but Piglet was afraid to admit to himself how good it made him feel to sense Pooh's delight in him. Instead, Piglet blushed and put himself down, saying, "Oh, No! Pooh. You shouldn't say 'O gallant Piglet,' because I did blinch a little. Just at first. And your song says, 'Did he blinch?' No, No!"

"You only blinched inside," said Pooh, "and that's the bravest way for a Very Small Animal not to blinch that there is."

Piglet glowed with happiness as he let himself think about himself being *brave*.

Just then, however, Eeyore (the donkey) rushed up to Pooh and Piglet announcing that he had just found the perfect house for Owl. (You see, Owl's house had blown down in the storm the night before.) So everyone hurried off to see the house that Eeyore had found. Imagine how Piglet felt when it turned out to be Piglet's very own house.

And then Piglet surprised himself. He did a noble thing. Still being in a daze thinking of all the wonderful words Pooh had sung about him, Piglet said, "Yes, it's just the house for Owl, and I hope he'll be very happy in it." And then Piglet gulped hard, because he had been happy in it himself.

Christopher Robin had joined them by this time, so Eeyore

asked, "What do *you* think, Christopher Robin?" Eeyore was uneasy, sensing that something was not quite right.

"Well," said Christopher Robin after thinking a long time, "it's a very nice house, and if your own house is blown down, you *must* go somewhere else, mustn't you, Piglet? What would *you* do, if *your* house was blown down?"

Before Piglet could think, Pooh answered for him. "He'd come and live with me, wouldn't you, Piglet?"

Piglet squeezed his paw. "Thank you, Pooh," he said, "I should love to."[4]

Piglet was indeed very big and very brave. Little Piglet, overlooked and neglected, pushed around and mistreated, dared to let himself be enjoyed by Pooh. He let Pooh make him feel brave and cared for. Even more risky, Piglet allowed himself to be generous toward Owl, and he let it happen spontaneously! Before he knew it, Pooh was inviting him to come and live with him. Then Piglet did the most courageous thing of all: he let himself be loved by his friend, Pooh. He said another spontaneous thing, the kind of thing he had longed to say to someone for his whole life: "Thank you, Pooh. I should love to."

Of course, Pooh had been in Piglet's neighborhood all the time. It's just that Piglet had not been ready. But now Piglet understood the words: "When you are ready, your guide will appear." Are you ready for a guide?

Part III
The Willingness
to Be Loved by God

6

The Courage to Believe in the Terrifying God

Piglet found that love is the remedy for fear. As we have just seen, he also found that it takes courage to be willing to be loved by a friend. For a fear-ridden person, it may take even more courage to be willing to be loved by God.

A person in the prime of life was surprised to realize that she was no longer torn by inner conflicts as she had been most of her early years. She was troubled, though, by the fact that she was not seeking God in prayer as often as she did during the years of unrelieved fears and inner pain. In telling a small group of trusted friends about it, she wondered out loud: "Maybe it's a good thing that I am not praying like I used to. Before, whenever I prayed, my praying was itself a fearful time. I could never be sure that my problems were not themselves a punishment from God. To be honest, the only God I knew was a terrifying God!"

A terrifying God? Yes. Perhaps you, too, know what it is to pray to a terrifying God—when trust is always at war with distrust, and God's love never feels unconditional. It is bad when, in seeking God, God is absent. It is worse when God is present—but terrifying.

Your Album of God Images

The courage *to believe* in a terrifying God is not easy to come by. A first step, however, is to realize that your personal picture of God is not necessarily the true God. The God picture in your mind may have been taken a long time ago. It is as if every child has a camera and takes pictures of the biggest and most powerful people in the house. Mainly, the child takes pictures when the big people are very intense about something or when the child is reacting to them in a strong way. Then the child looks at the pictures for awhile, takes out crayons and paper, and draws a picture of God. Only the camera and crayons are inside the child's mind forming the child's primitive image of God.

By the time you went off to kindergarten, you had drawn your own private picture. You constructed it from your feelings about the powerful people around you, from your own feelings about yourself, and from the beliefs you had been taught. Once formed, your God image was glued into your picture album of memories and cannot be made to disappear. It can be repressed and so forgotten, but as we have seen already, what is repressed does not die. Rather, it lies in ambush. If your first picture is only of a terrifying God, it will continue to harass you, to make your life miserable. But if you let your God image change and grow as you grow up, you will gain the courage to be loved—even by a terrifying God.

Jeremiah's Pictures of God

Jeremiah stands out as an example of a person whose God image changed even though his life was a story of rejection, abuse, and bitter disappointment. Few prophets are as revered in the Judeo-Christian story as Jeremiah. He is the great proclaimer of the new covenant (Jer. 31:31-34), the prophet of the single heart, and the one way with God (32:38-41). He pointed to the plans of God for those who truly seek the Lord (29:11-14). He showed what it means to be an authentic prophet (28:9) and what it means to be a false shepherd of God's people (23:1-4). No one saw more clearly that every promise of

God contains a built-in warning against disobedience. And he defined more specifically than anyone else in the Old Testament that a prophecy is valid only if the conditions remain the same (18:7-10). Jeremiah was undoubtedly one of God's great messengers.

Yet the personal life of Jeremiah is one of the Bible's saddest stories of loneliness and struggle with God. As the book opens Jeremiah begged not to be selected as a messenger for God. He realized that being a servant of God was not going to be a popular role in his society. He pleaded with God that he was too young for the task (1:6). God answered by giving him a series of judgment messages. Jeremiah tried hard to be faithful in delivering these devastating sermons, but they fell on deaf ears and he himself was spurned by his own people.

In utter helplessness and frustration he turned to God and asked him, "Why have you deceived me?" (20:7). What kind of a God are you that makes people laugh at me when I proclaim judgment (vv. 7-8)? I end up in the stocks (v. 2) and the people think I am stupid (v. 10). They all consider that my God is dead (v. 11). Jeremiah hated his task of proclaiming a terrifying God. Indeed, he cursed the day of his birth and he questioned his entire existence (vv. 14-18). If ever there was a potential candidate for suicide, it should have been Jeremiah. His picture of God appeared to be totally wrong to everyone. Indeed, as the story progressed, the people imprisoned Jeremiah in a muddy pit hoping that his words about a terrifying God of judgment would also be imprisoned (38:1-6). But as the time continued to move, Jeremiah's picture of God became far more realistic to the people than they could have imagined. As Babylon began its destructive march, judgment was no longer impossible to perceive (40:1ff.).

In the midst of this tragedy, however, Jeremiah began to speak a new message of hope. His picture of God was being enlarged and Jeremiah wanted the people to hear about the love of God in spite of judgment. The people, however, refused to listen to their prophet. In their anger at him, they carried him as a protesting prisoner to Egypt, despite the fact that he had warned them they would perish if they fled to the land of the Nile. As they refused to accept Jeremiah's God of judgment, they also refused to hear about the God of love. Thus they missed the prophecy of new hope as well (42:9-17; 43:5-7).

The amazing fact of Jeremiah's story is that in spite of his constant rejection by the people, his picture of God continued to develop. While his opponents retained simplistic pictures of God, Jeremiah's understanding grew. At first Jeremiah was indeed a messenger of a God who was harsh in judgment. He realized that Israel had failed God and needed a stern warning. But as the story continued, one sees the emergence of hope in the midst of judgment. Jeremiah began then to proclaim the love of God. It was not a spineless love, however, because the people of God were required to repent and become obedient. Unfortunately, the opponents of Jeremiah refused to open their minds to a big picture of God and so they perished, carrying with them their weeping prophet.

The Book of Jeremiah is filled with many aspects of tragedy concerning Israel's relationship to God. Yet it became for the people of God who survived the Babylonian captivity a word of hope and promise. In it are promises about the coming Messiah and forceful messages of God's covenant to be written on the hearts of His people. The Book of Jeremiah is the balanced message of a person who had experienced the greatness of God both in judgment and in mercy. It is a book that presents one of the fullest pictures of God in the Old Testament. The picture of God in this book contains messages both of assurance and warning, both of love and judgment. It is an inspired text which should be inwardly digested by every servant of God in the twentieth century. We need Jeremiah's big picture of God!

Revising Your God Image

What can you do with your image of God? You can update that image again and again, at each new stage of your growth. In fact, to be emotionally and spiritually healthy, you should be prepared to fill up a whole album with your changing God images. A person's private God image seldom fits the picture of God that we have in Jesus Christ. One way to understand spiritual growth, therefore, is to see it as filling an album of God pictures until the pictures in your private album become more and more like the picture of Jesus in the Bible. This way of seeing spiritual growth is suggested by Paul in the passage: "And we all, with unveiled face, beholding the glory of the Lord, are being changed into his likeness from one degree of glory to another; for this comes from the Lord who is the Spirit" (2 Cor. 3:18).

A good way to recall the God images in your album is to take a piece of paper and rule off ten vertical lines across the page as outlined in figure 1.

Now in the first column on the left, "Years from Birth," list the calendar years from the year of your birth to the present. (You may want to number in two-, three-, or five-year intervals.) In the last column on the right, "Ages," list your chronological age, from birth to your present age.

Next, in "Place of Residence," list geographical or address changes as they occurred, and, if you wish, economic and social "place" as well.

"Key Relationships" refers to people who have had a big influence on your self-image or sense of worth. They may be parents, siblings, friends, enemies, lovers, spouses, teachers, bosses, etc.

"Uses and Roles of Self" may include attending schools, developing skills and talents, taking on roles and responsibilities.

"Marker Events" are turning points in your life. They may be associated with geographical moves, deaths of loved ones, or religious events; marriage, separations or divorce; changes in status or role, etc.

"Events in the World" calls for attention to things going on outside your family and friendship circles. Such things as depression, wars, human rights campaigns, and the like provide a larger social perspective on the formation of your God image.

THE UNFOLDING TAPESTRY OF MY LIFE
Adapted from "Life Tapestry" © Center for Faith Development

Years from Birth	"Place" of Residence	Key Relationships	Uses & Roles of Self	Marker Events	Events in the World	Centers of Value	Authorities	Images of God	Age

Figure 1

"Centers of Value" call for you to name the causes that have been of such significance in your life that they have had an organizing power on all your other values. They may be relationships, roles, institutional loyalties, movements, etc.

"Authorities" asks for the person or group to whom you look for guidance or for primary approval of your decisions, choices, and values at a particular time of your life. Pay attention to times of shifting from one source of authority to another.

"Images of God" is the column for naming the pictures in your private album. These may be positive or negative; they may suggest God's presence or absence, belief or disbelief.

The "Age" column on the right enables you to orient your story to your age as well as to calendar years.

Fill in each column from your birth year to the present, recording just the central events and key people in your life. In this way you should be able to put your whole life story on one large page (or two at the most). Now take time to review the whole. Read across the columns in time periods and down each column as well. Allow your story to sink into your awareness as a whole. Then imagine that the story is a drama that needs to be divided into separate acts. Allow the story to fall into as many acts as necessary to mark off the major divisions, and draw heavy lines horizontally across the page to divide them.

Take time now to reflect on each act. Open yourself to the feelings you have about a given period of your life. Accept your feelings for what they are, whether pleasure or pain. Then try to give each act a title that says what you sense that act was about, what it means to you as you look back at it. The title may be a symbol, a metaphor, a key word.

Now review your life map once more. This time concentrate on your images of God. Compare each image of God with the other items on the horizontal line within a given act. In act I, does the image of God fit your self-image, your central authorities, the key relationships, for example? As you progress to act II and act III, does your God image change to reflect the marker events and the shifts in authorities? Are world events reflected in the struggles associated with your God image? Are your centers of value compatible with your God image or do they appear not to be connected internally? Wherever you find a God image that does not seem to match the quality of your life in other areas put a big X across the entry.

The next step in this review of your life story is to write at the very bottom of the page (or on a separate page that you attach to your story page) these words from Galatians 5:22-23,25. "The fruit of the Spirit is love, joy, peace, patience, kindness, goodness, faithfulness, gentleness, self-control; against such there is no law. If we live by the Spirit, let us also walk by the Spirit."

Examine your current God image in the light of the biblical description of the fruits of the Spirit. If your present God image does not produce these fruits in your experience, put a big X over all the entries in the final act of your story.

Next, imagine yourself with a God image that produces the fruits of the Spirit and write it in under "Images of God." Examine each of the other columns of your final act and imagine how the other items could become different in such a way as to reinforce your newly envisioned God image. Try not to feel bound by present limitations. Give yourself permission to imagine different key relationships, uses of self, centers of value, and authorities, all of whom would support a more positive and fruitful God image. What you are doing is seeing in your mind's eye the possibilities for the next act in your life's drama and opening yourself to an image of God that is more nearly like the God revealed in Jesus Christ.

You may want to come back to the above task several times over the next few days. Allow time for your memories to fill in the gaps and for a sense of your own drama to become clear. Putting together a picture album that tells the story of a lifetime should not be rushed. Completing it promises a sense of satisfaction and rich new understandings of the journey you have taken to this point in time.[1]

The basic assumption in asking you to pay attention to your God images is that a person's private picture of God is a strong force in shaping one's life story. God images that keep pace with the changes in growing up, that take account of the unexpected roadblocks and detours on the journey, and at the same time are "changed into (Christ's) likeness from one degree of glory to another" make for health and fulfillment. God images that are not revised in this way become either ridiculous and irrelevant or threatening and dangerous. The failure to nurture the growth of your God image can leave you trapped in the universe with only the experience of a terrifying God. But given the willingness to be loved, the terrifying God can also become for you a trustworthy God.

Willing to Be Loved: Paul's Call and His
New Image of God

One can identify the picture of a person's God by the way that person acts. This fact is clearly evident in the story of Saul/Paul. Saul breathed out threats and killed the Christians with the approval of the high priest (Acts 9:1). Luke indicated to his readers that Saul was the personification of terror in the name of religion. Saul's view of God must have been that of a stern vindictive deity who would exterminate anyone that got in His way.

With respect to a person like Saul, sometimes God finds that the most effective way to treat a misdirected religious firebrand is to stop him cold in his tracks. And God did just that to Saul. God struck Saul blind and informed him that his firebreathing activity against the disciples of Jesus was, in fact, directed against the God he thought he was serving (vv. 4-5). To say that the firebreather was shocked by the incident is a huge understatement. Luke tells us that Saul did not eat or drink anything for three days (v. 9).

Then Saul experienced his second shock. God sent one of the Christians that the persecutor was bent on exterminating to be a channel of the Holy Spirit and to bring him to a spiritual awakening. It requires little imagination to picture the anxiety that the Christian, Ananias, must have felt when God sent him to lay his hands on the persecutor, Saul (vv. 13-14). But the love of God reached down to Ananias and gave him courage. Then the love of God reached through Ananias to Saul. And God transformed the murderous exterminator into a preacher of the gospel of love who quickly amazed the citizens of Damascus (vv. 20-21). As the scales fell from his eyes (v. 18), Saul's picture of God was radically transformed. The persecutor who served a God he thought was intolerant of Christians became the proclaimer of the Jesus Christ (v. 22) who loved the world and died to bring humans into a right relationship with God.

This transformed Saul is the same Paul who could write in Philippians that while he had been blameless according to the requirements of the law, he regarded all of his former attempts at perfection as the equivalent of a garbage or manure pile in comparison to the marvelous blessing of coming to know Christ Jesus his Lord (3:4-8)! Discovering the gracious acceptance by God that is received through faith was for Paul an experience that literally banished his old views of God (v. 9). The willingness to suffer with Jesus, therefore, was not a sign of weakness for Paul but a deeply held conviction that the resurrection of Christ was both the most powerful event that the world had ever known and the sign of a Christian's eternal hope (vv. 10-11).

Paul was transformed when he met Jesus. Paul's little image of God was stretched beyond recognition. His transformation changed the entire way he went about serving God. Moreover, instead of being a persecutor, he himself became the object of persecution. Paul became a model of what it means for Christ to be alive in a person. Indeed, he charged the Philippians to imitate him and choose as examples for emulation other models of self-giving love like himself (v. 17). His willingness to be a model was not a matter of personal pride. He knew that his own model was none other than the self-giving Jesus Himself. Indeed, Paul reached one of the high points of all his teaching when, in beautiful poetry, he pointed to Jesus as the perfect model and called on all Christians to have the mind of Christ Jesus (see 2:5-11).

Paul's willingness to be loved by Christ and to be led by the Spirit continued to flower throughout his life. As he came to the end of his time on earth, he clearly affirmed that he had "kept the faith" and that he was genuinely prepared for his "departure" (2 Tim. 4:6-7). He wanted the Christians not to be ashamed either of his sufferings or of the witness of Christ (1:8). Instead they should be ready to suffer and be prepared to remain fully committed to the gospel, which was the basis for his own calling (vv. 10-11). Furthermore, the model of Christ's self-giving became for Paul the foundation of his readiness to endure all things for the sake of the people of God (2:10).

The apostle to the Gentiles experienced the power of God's love in a person like Ananias. Then in accepting the model of Jesus' ultimate self-giving, Paul himself became the embodiment of this self-giving love. Such unselfish love is the key that opens the heart of people to a new willingness to be loved. It is the genuine context for true freedom in the Lord and for the courage to reenvision our puny pictures of God.

The Secret of a Prayer Rug

Out of another ancient tradition comes a parable about a tinsmith who was unjustly imprisoned. He was allowed to receive a rug woven by his wife. Day after day he prostrated himself on the rug to say his prayers. After some time he said to his jailers:

"I am poor and without hope, and you are wretchedly paid. But I am a tinsmith. Bring my tin and my tools and I shall make small artifacts which you can sell in the market, and we will both benefit."

The guards agreed to this, and presently the tinsmith and they were both making a profit, from which they bought food and comfort for themselves.

Then one day, when the guards went to the cell, the door was open and he was gone.

Many years later, when this man's innocence had been established, the man who had imprisoned him asked him how he escaped, what magic he had used. He said:

"It is a matter of design, and design within a design. My wife is a weaver. She found the man who had made the locks of the cell door, and got the design from him. Then she wove the design into the carpet, at the spot where my head touched in prayer five times a day. I am a metal worker, and this design looked to me like the inside of a lock. I designed the plan of the artifacts to obtain materials to make the key—and I escaped.[2]

To allow this parable of the tinsmith to open its secrets to you, ask yourself, "What is the prison in which I find myself unjustly confined." Is it a prison of fears that are rooted in my genetic inheritance? My early childhood years of cruelty and pain, abandonment or abuse? A crippled body? My addictions to overwork, to worry, to overindulgence in eating, drinking, sex, gambling, spending money, shoplifting? Is my prison being hypercritical, lying, daydreaming? Is it being moody, self-pitying, bitter, greedy, impulsive, selfish?

Now ask yourself, "What is the prayer rug into which is woven the secret design for the lock that holds me prisoner?" The design you need in order to unlock your prison door has to do with your inner life—with the way you have been created by God. Once you see into the secrets of your own being and your relation to God—the true God, revealed in Jesus Christ, not your faulty god images from childhood—God will help you fashion the key that will set you free.

Notice in the parable that the prayer rug was received as a gift from the prisoner's wife. It was she who discerned the inner design of the lock. It was she who wove the design into the prayer rug. All that was required of the prisoner was to use the prayer rug many times a day. In using the prayer rug, the prisoner discovered the design for himself without a word being spoken. So, knowing the identity of the giver of the rug is equally as important as being able to recognize the rug when you see it.

Is it possible that the rug is the Word of God and the giver of the rug is God, the Holy Spirit? Is the secret design in your hands already, only waiting for you to be willing to receive it in your heart? Is it possible that the terrifying god of your fear-ridden heart is also the gift-giving God of whom Jesus spoke when he said: "What father among you, if his son asks for a fish, will instead of a fish give him a serpent; or if he asks for an egg, will give him a scorpion? If you then, who are evil, know how to give good gifts to your children, how much more will the heavenly Father give the Holy Spirit to those who ask him!" (Luke 11:11-13). Moreover, Paul reminded us: "The Spirit searches everything, even the depths of God" . . . and "no one comprehends the thoughts of God except the Spirit of God" (1 Cor. 2:10-11). Who else could know the secrets of your inmost self except the God of wisdom? How else could the design be revealed, except by the Spirit of God? Where else is the heart of God better revealed than in the person of Jesus? And how can you know Jesus better than to meditate day and night on the Jesus story in Scripture and to risk living in the midst of a community of genuine Jesus people?

Notice, also, that the prisoner of the parable remained in captivity for quite a long time after having discovered the secret design by which to escape. Your house of fears will hold you prisoner until you gain the tools and the materials for making a key with which to turn the lock. This is your part of a successful prison break. The Holy Spirit gives you the gift—the design for deliverance. The Word of God in Scripture, in the godly community, and supremely incarnate in Jesus, makes the design visible to the person who has eyes to see it. Once the design is seen, God Himself will help you to fashion the key for your own escape—your authentic freedom as a Christian.

Here, however, is the *big surprise*. The key that is forged in the design of God is to enable you to turn away from your fears and to aid you in your willingness to be loved by God. Jesus' way of introducing this reality was to announce: "The time is fulfilled, and the kingdom of God is at hand; repent, and believe in the gospel" (Mark 1:15).

Believing in the gospel does not mean that you will be free from doubt. Unamuno knew that the gift-giving God and the terrifying God are, in fact, the One True God:

Those who believe they believe in God,
but without passion in the heart,
without anguish of mind,
without uncertainty,
without doubt,
and even at times without despair,
believe only in the idea of God,
and not in God Himself.

Being in prison is a horrible plight—terrible evil—but, in the words of Abraham Heschel, "Evil is not [your] ultimate problem. [Your] ultimate problem is [your] relation to God." At the heart of your relation to God is the choice that only you can make: a choice to trust your distorted god image and draw back in fear or to trust the gospel—the good news of Jesus Christ—and be willing to be loved, even to be loved by the terrifying God. The willingness to be loved is so central in getting free from fear that it becomes the pulsebeat of the next several chapters. Only the willingness to be loved by God, terrible though God may be, releases the courage to die to fear, to risk community, and to live in the light of truth, empowered by a fearless love.

7

The Courage to Die to Fear and Be Reborn

Every stage of growth faces you with the choice to risk going forward into the unknown or drawing back in fear. The choice is more than a psychological decision about growing up. It is a matter either of living by faith or of shrinking back in unbelief. The expressions "living by faith" and "shrinking back in fear and unbelief" are key ideas which are at the heart of human life and at the core of the biblical message.

The Faith to Believe or the Fear of Shrinking Back

To live by faith has been God's way for people in both the Old and New Testaments (see, for example: Hab. 2:4; Rom. 1:17; Gal. 3:11). This idea of living by faith formed the trumpet call of the Protestant Reformation as indicated in Luther's famous expression *sola fide*—faith alone! But in emphasizing living by faith, Luther never forgot that there was another side to the expression, namely *sola gratia*—grace alone! The combination of these two expressions really provides us as Christians with the true meaning of living by faith. To live by faith is to live through God's marvelous grace by faith. Therefore, to live by faith is to believe (in spite of your fears) that the perfect love of God is with you in the human, tension-filled adventure of growing up.

To live by shrinking back in fear, however, is quite the opposite. It is to reject the graciousness of God's love in your life.

100

Shrinking back in fear is what the Bible calls unbelief. Unbelief is not merely a matter of a person's intellect rejecting some information about God. Unbelief involves turning away from reliance on the way of God. It is rebuffing God or disobedience (compare Rom. 11 and Heb. 3—4). Repentance, as we indicated earlier, therefore, means a turning around to live by faith or to live in a state of depending on the love of God.

Living by faith is the epitome of living courageously. But living courageously is woven into the very fabric of human existence. The courage to live by faith is the stuff of growing up. Think about your own life story for a moment. As an infant, you had to be brave enough to risk the bumps and hurts of falling in order to learn to walk. To enter the outside world of school, you had to venture outside the security of the home. Perhaps, at times you shrank back. Children often feign illnesses, for example, in their struggle between faith and unbelief, not knowing if they can trust the currents of life to carry them forward into the new adventures of growing up. The choice between faith and fear is made over and over again at every new stage of growth: in leaving childhood for adolescence, in giving up the immunities of the teens for the new freedoms and responsibilities of adulthood, and so on.

Now, at every transition in growing up a kind of death, burial, and resurrection takes place within a person. You die to the familiar and safe ways of the old stage of growth. As you let go of the old ways, allowing them to be buried in your memory, you can be reborn to new ways—to new freedoms, new relationships, and new discoveries about yourself and your world. The more successful you are in letting go of the old way and mastering the tasks of the new stage, the less fearful you will be at the next stage and those stages which follow thereafter. Accordingly, the story of growing up becomes a retelling, over and over again, of the infant's initial adventure in being forced out of the safety of the womb and into the vastness of hitherto unknown space with new and expanded freedoms, such as those of the delivery room, the hospital, and, ultimately, the whole wide world. So, the birth event opens a window through which you may be able to glimpse vistas of the inner, spiritual reality of your own life story more clearly than before.

A Perspective on Sin

At this point in our discussion of birth and growth it is well to be reminded of the story of Adam and Eve in the garden (Gen. 3) and of an erroneous conclusion sometimes drawn from that text. This inspired story is not meant to suggest that the "fall" so defaced the "image of God" in humanity that people are totally deformed with absolutely nothing good left in them. If such were the case, then human beings would hardly be worth redeeming. But the very opposite is, in fact, true. Yet old theological formulations such as "total depravity" tend to be misunderstood by many people today. Total depravity does not mean that all humans are little more than animals and are totally sinful. Instead, the biblical view is that everyone struggles with sinfulness. In the presence of God you need to recognize, like Isaiah, that you are from a people of unclean lips (Isa. 6:5); but God still can communicate with you. In spite of sin there are still amazing possibilities for becoming more and more godlike in your life through the gift of God's love. The reality of sin and the nature of faith point you to your need for living courageously with God rather than shrinking back into fearful, sinful ways of disobedience. Like the stages of your human life you need to experience the marvels of growth and rebirth in your spiritual life.

The Spiritual Reality of Believing

In your quest to understand the great spiritual realities of life, you have perhaps no better introduction than the Gospel of John. The purpose statement of that Gospel makes clear how John wanted his Gospel to be understood. "Many other signs Jesus did . . . which are not recorded in this book; but these are recorded in order that you might believe that Jesus is the Christ, God's Son, and that through believing you might have *life* in [or by] his name" (John 20:30-31).* Nothing less than genuine, wholehearted life believing is adequate to describe John's spiritual goal for his readers.

But this believing is not merely related to head knowledge. In order to make his point absolutely clear in the Greek, John never used the nouns for belief *(pistis)* or knowledge *(gnōsis)* in his Gospel. He used only verbs such as believing *(pisteuō)* and knowing *(ginōskō, oida)*. This fact stands out as unique in this Gospel, since earlier Paul had already frequently used such nouns. Why then did John write in such a strange way?

The reason seems to be that by the time John wrote his Gospel to the early church there was a growing heretical tendency among people to talk about spiritual reality in terms of "what one knows" rather than "who one knows." John was going to make absolutely sure that his readers understood that Christianity is not merely a matter of doctrine or *information* about God and the human situation. But Christianity is primarily a matter of being *related to the person* of Jesus and to *living* a life of loving obedience with God. In other words, John realized that people could perish or still go to hell in spite of the fact that they might affirm information *about* God and statements of doctrine *about* Jesus.

Living and believing in Jesus is different than repeating words about Jesus. Notice then how John even plays with the Greek words for *believing* and *knowing* in order to alert his readers that they needed to think specifically about the real nature of knowing and believing. He made the point that at Passover time "many Jews believed *(pisteuō)* in him" but that "Jesus did not believe or entrust *(pisteuō)* himself to them because he knew" or understood in the depth of relationships "what was in humanity" and he did not need superficial human testimonies to indicate what humans are like (John 2:23-25).

Moreover, John added in chapter 6 that, when the disciples really began to understand that believing in Jesus might lead to the necessity of a very deep commitment (vv. 52-59), they began to murmur (v. 61) like the people of Israel in the wilderness. They were not prepared to accept the fact that true believing is not the result of human effort but arises from the presence of God's Spirit in the life of a person (v. 63). The consequence was that many disciples shrunk back" in unbelief (v. 66). Indeed, Jesus even asked the disciples whether they would also shrink back in fear when the pressures would become great. Peter answered for the disciples that they could not depart because they had truly come to believe that Jesus was the Holy One of God and that He had the divine words of eternal life (vv. 68-69). But Jesus' question was not just an idle query. As the story continued, Peter proved later what insight Jesus possessed, because the strength of Peter's believing crumbled into fearful shrinking back and denial in the face of the hostility around the charcoal fire (18:15-27). So too, your task now is to get beyond the fear of shrinking back and return to the nature of birthing a life of believing.

Before Birth, the Labor Room

Pregnancy, labor, and delivery are stages in every birth. There is no way in a normal birth process to move from a full-term pregnancy to delivery of a new life without going through labor. Similarly, in being born anew spiritually, from a fear-ridden way of being in the world to a fearless love bond with God, you must go through the labor room of anxiety and fear.

Are you prepared to allow the birth analogy to speak to you

of your inmost self? If you are, you could come face-to-face with an exceedingly critical moment in your search for freedom from fear. Some people miss the point of birthing by thinking about being born anew spiritually merely as a one-time event. Of course, your first experience of being born anew needs to remain a treasured memory. But it also needs to point the way through the many crises in your spiritual life that are yet to come. The formula of pregnancy, labor, and delivery spotlights the path through each new stage of growth, and it can help us to hold a steady course through the anxiety and pain of inner transformations. It can provide the key to deliverance in the great crises of life when fear tends to mask the face of evil.

In the skillfully constructed third chapter of John's Gospel, which contains the most-quoted verse in the New Testament (v. 16), Jesus is pictured as using birth language with Nicodemus in order to unveil to him the mystery of spiritual awakening. As the story began, Nicodemus came to Jesus by night (v. 2). Notice that such designations in John are more than mere time notations. Nicodemus, the teacher, who thought he had Jesus all figured out—"we know" (v. 2)—was really in darkness and soon discovered that he was totally bewildered by Jesus' references to new birth. All Nicodemus could think about was the impossibility of climbing back into his mother's womb (v. 4). The absurdness of such a literal interpretation brought a needed clarification from Jesus that such new birth did not come by natural processes but came by water and the Spirit (v. 5).

Unfortunately, Nicodemus's thinking at this point was stuck in the earthly realm of making babies. Thus, even when Jesus tried to explain that birth language could be applied to the realm of the Spirit, Nicodemus repeated his bewildered question of "how . . . ?" (v. 9). At this point Jesus abandoned His patient approach and finally asked Nicodemus the incisive question of whether he as a teacher of Israel was not in fact blind to the realities which pertain to spiritual life (v. 10). Birth language can be a powerful symbolic vehicle for communicating realities far beyond the experience of the female womb. Like the symbolism of marriage which has been used by religious people to describe intimate relationships in the spiritual realm (compare Paul's use of the marriage relationship in Eph. 5:21-33), birth language is a ready-made symbol for picturing the beginning or the coming to a new awareness of a deeper stage in the reality of the Spirit.

Both Earthly and Heavenly Things

Jesus spoke to Nicodemus of earthly things hoping to open the eyes of his heart to heavenly things. We have written of earthly things in our discussion of human development. But our concern goes far beyond human development. Our desire is to open your eyes and to quicken your courage to risk discipleship in a new way. The story of your development as a child or adolescent may be one of repeated failure at the transition points of growth. You may have come through stage after stage without ever burying the old. Thus, you may have lived through your years without ever knowing the powers and joys of death and resurrection in each new phase of your life. You may be carrying with you a bagfull of fears from childhood and another bagfull from adolescence. Perhaps you have loaded on another bag of fears from marital or parental failures. If so, the developmental solutions to fear offer you nothing but even deeper discouragement. The gospel alternative—the good news!—in the life of discipleship is a promise that offers what developmental stages have failed to provide.

A Narrow Gate and a Hard Way

Jesus described the entrance into discipleship as a "narrow gate." But most people choose instead the wide gate and the easy way "that leads to destruction." Unfortunately, according to Jesus, few people find the narrow gate and the hard way associated with it. But it is the path "that leads to life" (Matt. 7:13-14). These words are true whether you are hunting for the gate that leads to life for the first time or whether you entered the narrow gate many years ago and are still struggling to die to fear and to be reborn in love in your movement from stage to stage on your spiritual journey.

Finding the narrow gate often takes on the marks of a spiritual emergency. Passing through the gate creates new crises resulting form the spiritual awakening. A four-stage journey brings you from your first frantic knocking on the gate, to the agony of dying to your old way, to the joy of having surrendered to the new way and being reborn a new self. Here then are the stages in the discipleship process, the journey through a narrow gate onto a hard way—the way of dying to fear and being reborn in the love that casts out fear.[1]

Stage 1: Finding the Gate

You find the gate by following your anxieties and fears. Surprising though it is, your fears will bring you to the gate in due time. You will reach a point at which you can no longer endure your fears alone. Something has to give. You come to a crisis point when you become more and more restless, confused, and fearful. You may be feeling helpless, uncertain, scared, and isolated. The fear of losing control is usually prominent as a person starts groping for the gate. Deep down inside, your self-esteem is wounded. You may be losing respect for yourself. You feel defeated, misunderstood, alone, and desperate.

Your anxiety becomes severe. You begin to look for ways to escape the inner pain. Nothing else matters. Anything seems better than going on. Psychic pain may be reaching panic proportions. Chaos is creeping in on all sides. Your suffering is intense. You feel stuck, lost, and hopeless. Inside you feel empty as if you are a nothing, a nobody.

Unknown to you, your anxiety and fear are leading you straight to the gate through which you may enter a new life. But then you veer to the left or to the right. If you veer to the left, you find yourself doing crazy and self-defeating things. You may be drinking too much, controlling those who are close to you too much, withdrawing too much, breaking the rules of sensible behavior too openly, too self-destructively. If you veer to the right, however, you will be in full flight back to the old ways, the way things used to be, in the hope that the simplistic rules and regulations of the past will save you from the suffering of the present.

At this point your most desperate need is to find a friend or a group of people who will help you bear the pain without drowning yourself in foolish behavior or running back to the old ways, the very ways that have failed you many times over and helped to bring you to the present crisis.

The friend you need may be a pastor, a chaplain, or a counselor. You may find that you can hold a steady course toward the gate in a self-help group. Most of all, you need to stay with your pain and chaos until it brings you to the gate. Usually things must get worse before they can get better. That is why it is so important not to give up the struggle by giving in to self-defeating behaviors or retreating to your former ways.

Stage 2: Crossing the Threshold

Things must get worse in order for you to be wiling to let go, to stop trying to run your own life, or to fix things by willpower. Finally you reach that point of no return. You give up trying to influence your own fate. You surrender to a Higher Power, whether you fully believe in it or not. And then the gate opens. The key that turns the lock is *surrender*.

Under the best of circumstances you know that you are surrendering to the God who created you, the God who has been pursuing you in your pain, the God who has become flesh and is one with you in your suffering, the God who is nothing like your old primitive God image. You surrender to the God who is known in the suffering love of Jesus of Nazareth.

Your surrender is a coming home to your true self—awakening to the image of God in which you were created. You may be flooded by the light and joy of being at peace with yourself and with God. You will certainly experience new energy and inner freedom from the conflicts and chaos of the past.

If you have made a discipleship decision earlier in your life, you may find it less dramatic to come once more to the gate of surrender than the preceding paragraphs suggest. Spiritual emergencies such as this may happen often in a person's life, however. They may happen at the times of transition from one age stage to another or they may be triggered by crises in your health, your marriage or family life, your employment, or in the world at large, such as by depression or war.

Stage 3: Hard Way

Crossing the threshold of the narrow gate can bring new problems. You can easily become inflated with the sense of your own importance. For awhile you may feel out of control under the surge of energy, joy, and love. You may threaten your friends by your enthusiasm. You should postpone any decisions that would make a major change in your life situation until your early excitement has calmed down and the impact of your spiritual awakening has had time to settle into a way of life.

You may be frightened by sensations of disintegration and death. Know that the outgrown parts of your old self are being discarded. Like the sloughing off of old skin, many aspects of your old life are dying and falling away. You are now in a time between the old and the new. It is a time of making sense as you make new discoveries about the riches of your inmost self.

But you will not feel altogether solid within. You must simply trust the process of change, knowing that you are being transformed by the Spirit of God who is actively at work within (2 Cor. 3:18).

Occasionally, a person discovers that their spiritual rebirth has awakened some unusual spiritual experiences. Visions of God in the form of Christ may confront you. The Spirit may appear in some other form, reassuring and frightening you at the same time. Such visitations may come in visual ways, or as the voice of God, or simply as an undeniable sense of the Divine Presence.

Again, you may discover that you are seeing things in your mind's eye and knowing things about the future without any reliance on your ordinary sensory ways of knowing. Such experiences are called clairvoyance when they involve seeing; clairaudience when they involve hearing; and clairsentience when they involve feeling what another is feeling, without direct contact or any ordinary means of communication. Glossolalia or speaking in tongues is another such experience. It often becomes a spontaneous form of prayer. It occurs rarely, however, for persons who have never been a part of a religious group that encourages this form of joyful praise to God. Some persons stumble upon the capacity for autonomic writing or speaking. In times of intense inner silence and concentration one may begin spontaneously to write or to speak. Your writing or speaking in the Spirit may be done with little conscious awareness on your part. Sometimes the words that are written or spoken will prove to be wise and useful to yourself and to others. Such words usually have poetic quality and serve the purpose of guidance in spiritual growth. You need to avoid being overly influenced by the uncommon origin of such messages. Remember that the apostle Paul carefully warned the Corinthians that the spirits of the prophets are subject to the prophets (1 Cor. 14:32). We do have a part in determining our experiences. Therefore, in the life of the Spirit, every message needs to be tested by the shared wisdom of the community of faith and against the revelations received through the Holy Scriptures.

All such experiences are familiar in the Bible and in the history of Christian spirituality. They can serve the purposes of comfort and guidance; they can open alternative ways of knowing; enable fervent and joyful prayer; and help a person get in touch with an inner wisdom not easily accessible otherwise. It is not unusual, however, for people to be frightened by the gifts of the Spirit. Some people looking on from outside the experience may be so fearful that they will tell you that your spiritual capacities are evil and should be totally avoided.

The apostle Paul was thoroughly familiar with the experiences that sometimes accompany spiritual awakenings. Concerning spiritual gifts, Paul wrote, "I do not want you to be uninformed." The gifts are for "the common good" of the church. But he cautioned sternly against being inflated with a sense of personal importance based on the gifts one has, and he summarized his views by urging the people in the church at Corinth earnestly to "desire the higher gifts" (1 Cor. 12:31). Moreover, he added that he wanted to show them a "superior way." Then Paul detailed the fact that love ought to form the style of the Christian life in the magnificent words of 1 Corinthians 13.

Paul's love chapter (1 Cor. 13) is the standard by which to measure every spiritual experience. Extra-normal powers of spiritual awareness are of no consequence at all, according to Paul's vision, unless they are used in the service of a mature love. Moreover, they may cause problems for the church unless they are employed wisely and orderly so as not to disrupt the extension of God's work (1 Cor. 14). Other New Testament writers encourage you to "test the spirits to see whether they are of God" (1 John 4:1). A wise test in this respect is the test of

the Great Commandment of Jesus: does the spiritual gift in-
crease wholehearted love of God and inspire love of your
neighbor as yourself (compare Matt. 22:37-40)? If you use
your visions to deepen your love for God and your experiences
of the Spirit to serve your neighbor, you need not fear. The goal
of Christian life is measured in terms of authenticity both
toward God and toward other people. Celebrate then the gifts
of God's grace in your life and joyfully use them in the service
of a maturing love for God and one another.

Jesus' favorite imagery for testing a person's spirituality is
the test of "fruits." He warned His disciples against "false
prophets" and said, "You will know them by their fruits"
(Matt. 7:15-20). The test of the fruit of the Spirit as developed
in the letter of Paul to the Galatians is most specific: "the fruit
of the Spirit is love, joy, peace, patience, kindness, goodness,
faithfulness, gentleness, self-control; against such there is no
law" (Gal. 5:22-23).

Another problem of a different kind may beset you in stage 3.
This is the backlash problem. After a few days or weeks of a
spiritual high following your breakthrough of surrender, you
can expect your old doubts and fears to swamp you like a tidal
wave once again. Your doubts may grown intense. You may
seek out old friends who will be all too glad to have you join
them in the familiar palaver of bitterness, sarcasm, ridicule of
religiousness, and the futility of higher aspirations.

In John Bunyan's *The Pilgrim's Progress*, Pilgrim and his
traveling companion, Pliable, started out on the journey to the
Celestial City with stars in their eyes about the joys ahead,
only to fall into the Slough of Despond. Pliable scrambled out
and ran back home to the City of Destruction, but Pilgrim
sank deeper and deeper into the swamp until Help (a Divine
Presence) gave him a hand and pulled him out. Help then
showed Pilgrim that he fell into the swamp because his eyes
were on the stars rather than on the ground in front of him,

causing him to miss the stepping-stones on which he might have picked his way through the Slough of Despond without falling in.

During a backlash time, you will do well to remember that your decision of surrender was conscious and intentional. You were wide-awake and aware of what you were doing. You made a free and unforced choice. As a responsible act, you were, and still are, willing to accept responsibility for the surrender, even if it should turn out to be a mistake. In being responsible for your surrender, you will not blame any other person, cause, force, or spiritual entity for it. You accept full responsibility for the consequences of your decision. Remember, also, that your surrender was directed to the true God. It cannot in any way be a means of furthering your self-importance. You simply gave your own soul to the ultimate mystery that created it, energizes and sustains it to this moment. You were not seeking an easy out, an escape from life, or a quick rise to fame. You were instead, with your whole heart, engaging the fullness of life with the fullness of yourself.[2]

To clarify for yourself what it was that you did in the process of surrender and to renew your commitment will go far toward lifting the fog that covers you while you wait for the tide of doubt and fear to go out again. Go out it will—for awhile that is. But the tide will come in again and again during stage 3, for this is the stage between the times. Do not be surprised if the next incoming tide carries a "Divine homesickness." The longing for the inner harmony, illumination, and freedom following your initial surrender may be so overwhelming and yet feel so far away, so out of reach, that you may be overcome by a temporary depression. You may feel quite powerless, without self-control, and even suicidal—feeling damned to failure in your spiritual adventure.

Times such as this force an inner collapse of your willpower, but simultaneously, they open you to receive divine aid coming from beyond yourself. Gradually you learn to trust the Spirit of God. You begin to relax the tension in your body and to let go of many of the old fears. In letting go of the fears you can begin to see that you clung to them and ruminated upon them because you actually needed them. You needed them for the cold comfort they gave you, assuring you that you were right in feeling fated to a life of misery—in seeing all of life as a cruel joke.

"Divine homesickness" may well be linked to the "blown-fuse" syndrome. A "blown fuse" results from putting too much drain on the energy supply. This happens when you try too hard to integrate the new experience of spiritual awakening. When you are impatient about the years it takes to complete a spiritual transformation, and when you do not want to put up with the rhythms of the tides—allowing barren periods to follow fertile ones. You may attempt spiritual heroics in an effort to force the changes for which you long. What you get is exhaustion rather than transformation. You may extend your periods of depression, suffer insomnia, mental agitation, restlessness, and a sense of guilt about your failure to live up to your ideals for a spiritually mature person.

In order not to continue to blow your inner fuses you need to accept the fact of rhythms in the life of the Spirit. Celebrate your times of spiritual renewal and vitality and be patient with yourself during the arid times. Enjoy the energies of love, joy, and peace when they are flowing and trust the empty spaces to be times of deep inner consolidation. Two images dominate the writings of Christian spirituality: the images of mountain and desert. Both are essential in spiritual growth. The mountains—symbolizing inspiration and communion with the Presence—stand in silent and necessary connection to the desert spaces below: spaces filled with absence, dryness, and barrenness.

As your new self emerges, gaining strength and stability, you may be uneasy about a sense of leading a "double life." The "double life" is the experience of attending to the everyday needs and business of life with a part of your awareness while secretly watching over your spiritual awareness and sustaining an inner spiritual discipline at the same time. For some, this happens as they commit themselves to use a prayer form such as model prayer of Jesus. While maintaining the inner ebb and flow of the prayer, you are going about your work, carrying on conversations, making decisions, and doing all the things needed of you. The experience is a bit like working on a highway construction crew in one lane of an expressway without stopping the flow of traffic in another lane. You set up the necessary structures to maintain the "double life" of the spirit, and you work at a measured pace that allows both levels of mental traffic to continue to flow simultaneously.

During stage 3 your number-one concern is to nurture your newborn spiritual awareness. You take advantage of workshops and training events in spiritual disciplines; you develop a plan for spiritual reading; and, most central of all, you sustain a regular time of silence, meditation, and centered prayer—a time given not to the struggle of spiritual achievement but to enjoying your Divine Lover in simply being together with delight in each other. You may do journaling or develop other disciplines that you find personally compatible. A good bit of trial and error must be part of this time of spiritual formation. Most crucial to your growth, however, is to seek and find a community of warm, loving, and faithful soul friends who share your excitement and struggles on the journey. It is at this point that you see the link to the next chapter, "The Courage to Risk Community." Before turning to the next chapter, however, the drama of spiritual pregnancy, delivery, and birth reaches its final act.

Stage 4: Dying to Fear, Reborn to Love

About the time you have forgotten your dreams of enjoying a stable state of God consciousness with relative freedom from the high and low tides of God's Presence and absence you waken to the realization that you are in another stage of your spiritual journey. One day it comes to you that you have a solid connection with your inmost self that has not gone soft or slippery on you for quite a while. You realize that you have made several decisions recently that were truly inner directed. You did so trusting your own path to be right for you. All of this has been happening with increased clarity and confidence about your life.

Simultaneously, you admit to yourself that you are more in touch with your own body and with the world of nature. You are awake to a strong concern to protect the birds, the animals, and the fish with whom we share both air and water for our survival. What surprises you, however, is that you are equally as concerned for the survival of the animal world as for the human world. Another surprise may be realizing that your health is improved without your having waged a campaign of any kind. For women, the health surprise includes freedom from a nicotine or caffeine addiction, compulsive overeating or overworking. In a word, you realize that without tearing at yourself, your will and your desire have become one, moved now by the love of God, of others, and of the whole created world.

Psychologically the new stage you have entered is known as a stage of self-realization. Theologically you are enjoying the fruits of sanctification, the freedom of the Spirit. The apostle Paul put it this way: "Now the Lord is the Spirit, and where the Spirit of the Lord is, there is freedom. And we all, with unveiled face, beholding the glory of the Lord, are being changed into his likeness from one degree of glory to another; for this comes from the Lord who is the Spirit" (2 Cor. 3:17-

18). Some of the characteristics of this stage of spiritual awakening are a more-than-normal level of euphoria: love, joy, and peace; a more-than-normal level of security, of being safe, cared for, sustained, and loved by God; a more-than-normal level of physical energy, endurance, and good health, frequently accompanied by the spontaneous remission of a disease process; a more-than-normal level of insight, of seeing meaning and purpose for life; and a heightened sense of an inmost and true self in which one is linked durably with God. The true self is known in contrast to an old false self which is not dead but is now weak and is at times, only a dim memory.

In stage 4, your work is to trust the evidences of the Spirit working within you and around you and to continue to allow the Spirit of God to guide your growth in the reborn life of love. A spiritual guide with whom you consult on a regular basis will help you discern the moving of the Spirit in your world and will join you in a mutual covenant of intercessory prayer. Often the best resources for such spiritual guidance are written in the small-group structures of a church.

Another temptation is to separate yourself from those who are struggling at earlier stages of the game, to feel spiritually superior. To allow your spiritual growth to become a source of feeling self-important is to forget that spirituality is a gift from God. Your best strategy for overcoming this temptation is to involve yourself in altruistic love and service of others. Genuine caring for others is both the fruit and the test of stage 4 living. In the struggle with both pride and fear, your ultimate resource is the perfect love of God. God's love is made perfect, however, in your loving care of others. At this stage you will find the following biblical words ringing true to your own experience:

> There is no fear in love, but perfect love casts out fear. For fear has to do with punishment, and he who fears is not perfected in love. We love, because he first loved us. If any one says, "I love God," and

hates his brother, he is a liar; for he who does not love his brother
whom he has seen, cannot love God whom he has not seen. And this
commandment we have from him, that he who loves God should love
his brother also (1 John 4:18-21).

The mystery of love such as this is never drained dry of its
awe and wonder, never emptied of its energizing power, never
idle in the process of generating within you the courage to die
to fear and the willingness to be reborn in love. Mechtild of
Magdeburg understood the inner reality of living in stage four
as well as anyone ever has. Among her words of wisdom, these
call out to sum up the process by which love overcomes fear in
all its forms:

> As love grows and expands in the soul,
>   it rises eagerly to God
>   and overflows
>   towards the Glory
>   which bends towards it.
> Then Love melts through the soul
>   into the senses,
> so that the body too might share in it,
> for Love
>   is drawn
>   into all things.[3]

8
The Courage to Risk Community

Belonging in the Story

The living heart of surrender to God is the courage to be in the story of the people of God, to risk being in community, to accept adoption into the family of God. The story of the people of God is God's story. It is not my story or your story. It is not the story of a family, a country, or a single denomination. It is not about a particular church or a set of beliefs. It is a tapestry that God is weaving century after century. It pictures all the races, all the persecutions and the religious wars, all the heroes and heroines, and all the people—forgotten or remembered—who have ever been on mission for God in the world.

Surrender to God means stepping into the river of God's story as it sweeps through human history. It means being carried away by the current of that river, but not to be drowned and lost. Only the puny and petty story of a person's self-centeredness is lost. In the strong current of God's story you are caught up in a little community of people shooting the rapids in a rubber raft on a white-water ride through life.

To be in the story is radically different from believing in the story. Many people believe the story, admire the art that pictures the story, thrill to the songs and hymns of the story, and, all the while, remain at a safe distance—in the balcony observing the story. To be in the story is to be on the set, in front of the cameras, actually living out a role in the story as it unfolds in your day and time. Your part in the story may be what the movie makers would call a "bit part." You may be part of a crowd scene, an "extra," but you are in the story all the same. You are involved. You are committed. You are exercising the courage to risk community with the people of God.

In the previous chapter, you saw a four-stage journey from acute fearfulness, through the narrow gate of surrendering yourself to God, onto a hard road of spiritual growth, until at last your will and your desire become one with perfect love. God's perfect love then casts out fear as a controlling power in your life. In a sense, this chapter expands the description of stage 3. It is about the time between the times of surrender to God and that glad day when you are no longer a slave to your fears.

Once you have exercised the courage to die to fear in surrender to God, you are ready to practice the courage to risk community. For it is in a community of warm, loving, and faithful soul friends who share your excitement and struggles on the journey that you find the food and training you need to grow spiritually. You discover that you are now part of the story of the people of God. Belonging in the story proves sufficient for being delivered from the terrors of the journey.

Becoming a Part of the Biblical Story

The Bible contains a series of pictures about those who accepted their roles in the great story of the people of God as well as those who found their lives out of sync with God's purposes. The story of God and His people is a story that began with Adam, moved with a somewhat erratic beat until the coming of our Savior, Jesus Christ, and still continues, even to the present and beyond. It is a two-sided story of failure and victory. But the central character of this story is not a David, or a Daniel. It is not even a Peter or a Paul. The hero of the Bible is God, His marvelous Son, and the Holy Spirit who is God's personal presence on earth. Human beings and the way they respond to God's leading are the focal points in the story, but not the prime movers.

In the biblical story, because of human sin, God has had to settle for a remnant of the people. God wanted the faithfulness of Adam and Eve, just as He wanted the obedience of Cain. But you know the sad story of how God has had to deal with human rebellion or, at its best, half-hearted human commitment. Yet God does not give up on the goal of bringing people to Himself and helping them find meaning and security.

When human rebellion seemed hopeless, God tried again to build a new humanity with Noah. But that attempt was hardly on its way when it faltered in the drunkenness of Noah and the debauchery of his son (Gen. 9:20-28). This pattern of evil continued until it reached judgment in the Tower of Babel story (Gen. 11:1-9).

Then God tried again to create a new community and to build the story through Abraham and his children. It too began to fail almost immediately with Abraham and Sarah. Yet God continued. Moreover, God did not demand that everyone in this story would be an exciting leader like Abraham. Extroverts are not the only people in this story. Some have been home body types like Isaac whose only major claim to fame is that he was part of the story. But we can never forget that Isaac has been part of this story and his part was also important.

The story does not only involve Israelite men, as if race or the male sex could tell the story by itself. Early in the story a Gentile prostitute by the name of Rahab found a place in the story (Jos. 2:1ff.; cf. Matt. 1:5 and Heb. 11:31). When Matthew penned his genealogy, he made it clear that both men and women are part of God's community story. Indeed, Matthew's inclusion of Tamar and Ruth (1:3,5) was undoubtedly pointed to remind his readers that women belong in this story. In the same manner, the mention of Uriah's wife was surely inserted to call to everyone's memory the contrast between the faithfulness of a Gentile Hittite and the sinfulness of Israel's revered King David (v. 6).

The story of the Old Testament thus can be written as a story of the faithfulness of God in spite of the faithfulness of many in the community. Nevertheless, throughout the story there was always a faithful remnant who struggled in the face of persecution to affirm the purposes of God. When Elijah thought he was the only one in the story, there was still a community (1 Kings 19:18). When the kings of Israel rejected God, there were still prophets like Hosea. When the people of God were carried off into Babylon and the story seemed to be finished, there was still a Daniel and a great visionary, Ezekiel, who saw from God that Israel was like a valley of dry bones that could come to life again (Ezek. 37).

With the coming of Jesus, the story gained a powerful new dimension of fulfillment in the working of God's saving purposes. The community that was born again through Jesus received the power of the Holy Spirit and a clear summons to proclaim the good news of salvation to all the world. But the world and the community are still not identical and the need for the story of God's redeeming people has become even more intense. Persecution and pain are still part of this new chapter which has been inscribed with the blood of the Lord Jesus, and has been affirmed with the lives and the deaths of His followers.

To have a part in this story is to discover the strength of the community despite human pain and hurt. It is to find in Christ and His people the power of God's Spirit which overcomes human loneliness, anxiety, and fear. It is to live with a history that testifies to the faithfulness of God. It is, likewise, to live with a future which confesses that Christ will come again and receive His people to Himself. And it is to live in the present with the ability to look in both directions and to have confidence in God and a spirit of love toward others. Eyes of faith can perceive both the story of the past and the hope of the future while living in the present. To live in this manner, seeing with eyes of faith, is to become part of the greatest story in the history of the world.

Seeing Others with New Eyes

Once you surrender to God, your personal story takes second place to *the* story of what God is doing in the world. Your eyes are opened to see the big story. Deep down you know that God is at work in everyone else as well as in yourself. With that knowledge you can begin to see other people in a new way. Your old knee-jerk reactions of fear, antagonism, or avoidance of people give way to curiosity about how God is dealing with the person who is there before you. You discover that in seeing *into* others in search of the tracks of the Spirit in their lives, you forget about being frightened of them; you feel less insecure and lonely. The more you sense your connectedness with others as children of the same loving God the less pressure you are under to attack them or try to drive them away.

Gradually, in a way that is so silent and subtle you may not be aware that the change is taking place, you see other people to be less threatening, less like storm clouds about to break on you, and more like a garden inviting you to enter, explore, and enjoy your time together.

Sometimes the gardens you enter in relationship with others are overgrown with weeds and thorns. You are sad to see the traces of paths no longer used, flowers being choked by neglect. You know you cannot stay long in the relationship. Neither can you tend the garden unless you are invited to do so. You may even be scratched and bleeding as you leave. On occasion you will be driven back from the garden gate.

Even though you are hurt by rejection, you partly understand. You remember the time before you crossed the gate of surrender when you were frightened of closeness, guarded, brittle, and struggling to keep up the appearance of being totally self-sufficient. Moreover, you know that the same Spirit that awakened you to newness of life is working in your frightened friend.

In 1957 Martin Luther King, Jr. met the hostility, rejection, and attacks of fear-ridden and vicious people by saying, "If you just keep on loving a man, ultimately you will get down to the God in him. . . . Ultimately, the most prejudiced mind in Montgomery, the most prejudiced mind in America, will become a loving mind. And twenty-five years from now men will look back and laugh." Twenty-five years later, in 1982, George Wallace was running for governor of Alabama again, confessing that enforced racial segregation was morally wrong.

Seeing and Caring Become One and the Same

Seeing "the God" in a person means caring about the person. And caring may be done even without speaking to a person or otherwise acting directly on them. Looking with loving eyes on a total stranger, offering them the gift of the delight in your eyes and the goodwill in your heart, is one way of being in the story of God's people. As a single wave on a lake or in the ocean has its own shape and fills its own place for a moment, but is connected with every other wave, arising out of the same source and returning to it, so you are connected with everyone else. So, too, your genuine impulse of longing love for another's welfare touches them. Just as a pebble tossed into a calm lake sends ripples that move every other molecule in the lake, so an impulse of spontaneous intercessory prayer touches everyone around you.

Spontaneous Intercession

Seeing with loving eyes and caring with a whole heart is the essence of intercession. Without intending to pray, you waken to the realization that you are engaged in intercession—spontaneously. Attentive love is the electric current of spirit upon spirit. As each member of the body is joined to the whole, so you are attached to the human family. Just as the pain of one member of your body touches you totally, so the healing power of your longing love for another touches them totally. Just as the joy of another delights you, so your own joy in the presence of the Spirit of God in your life wakens others to long for the Spirit of God in themselves. Teilhard de Chardin asked, "What is the work of works for [people] if not to establish, in and by each one of us, an absolutely original center in which the universe reflects itself in a unique and inimitable way? And those centers are our very selves and personalities."[1] And those centers, furthermore, are the power centers by which the Spirit of God keeps the story unfolding from one person to another and from one generation to the next.

Intentional Intercession

Charles Whiston opens his work on the simplicity, the power, and the wonder of intentional intercessory prayer with these words: "God cares, and cares redemptively for each and every . . . creature. . . . But it is only slowly over the years that we learn . . . that caring is not Christian caring until it is caring for all. We are encouraged in Scripture to "pray constantly" (1 Thess. 5:17), but neither the call to pray constantly nor to "care for all" is possible so long as prayer is understood as a formal, religious act, such as one does in church. Whiston brings intercession within reach of everyone in saying, "All that we need to do is to turn our hearts toward God; name the person; then offer to God our loving and unselfish concern for that person."

Even without naming the person, intercession may take place. You may notice a person passing by on the street or sit-ting across from you on a bus or in an airplane. You sense their need without understanding it, and your heart goes out to them. You look upon them with loving eyes. And you know that the Spirit of God is making intercession for them "with sighs too deep for words" (see Rom. 8:26-27).

Whether named or unnamed, those for whom your heart goes out in prayer are touched by God's Spirit. We know that God cares for every person, and so we cannot believe that God is indifferent to our offering when we give our love and energy to another of God's creatures. Just how God uses our gift of care for others is not ours to control, but the evidence that intercession has real consequences mounts up the more we continue to give ourselves to it. William Temple is said to have replied to a reporter who asked if he believed in intercessory prayer, "I cannot say whether intercessory prayer is effective or not. I can only say that when I begin to pray, remarkable coincidences start to happen." Whiston documented some of those consequences:

> This work of intercession has very real consequences. The first and foremost result is that it actually conforms us to God's redemptive concern for all. We find our lives sharing more and more in God's love for all. We find ourselves living less and less for ourselves, and like God, living more and more for others. We find that we are given by God deeper and truer insight into the real needs of those for whom we intercede. We enter into richer and fuller companionships with people, just because they are rooted in praying.[2]

We know, too, that there are real and objective effects upon those for whom we intercede. In the life of the Christian community person after person tells a story of hidden intercession—unknown to the person at the time—but intercession that was linked with the person's salvation, with healings, and with breakthroughs of freedom from fear. So, Whiston added, "we are . . . given through intercession a much deeper insight into the essential meaning of the

Church—that great fellowship of all those whose lives are knit together by God in Jesus Christ."[3]

A Personal Testimony

I knew this Charles Whiston before he died. When I first met him he seemed to be a little spooky. He wanted people to learn to pray; and, with my upbringing, I was sure that I knew how to pray. But then he invited me to a silent prayer retreat. It was the first time I had ever spent twenty-four hours (!) in total silence with God, but I knew I could do it even though most of the people I knew would start to squirm in their pews after the first minute and a half of silence. In this and other experiences I learned many years ago along with other seminary professors not to be afraid of the discipline of silence because we can really meet God in the silence.

Do you know what it is like to pray for an hour telling God all that is on your heart? Do you know what it is like to go the second, the fourth, and the sixth hours? Do you know what it is like to run out of things to say to God? Then do you know what it is like to start to listen, to hear the sounds of the world, to hear the voice of God in the midst of the world, to sense the heartbeat of God in the breathing of other persons, to realize that in the great as well as in the very tiny movements of the world our God is present. Have you really learned what it is like to be at peace with God in the world? In the years that followed that first experience there have been for me other times of silence, some much longer; but I will never forget the ending of my fear of silence in that first experience in a silent prayer retreat.

I also heard Charles thank God for water that you can drink when you turn on the tap. He had been in China for many years and he had learned to thank God for simple things. I too remember my first experience when I came back from an extended trip where I could find little bottled water, let alone tap water. And what water I found had fizz. Do you know what it is like to have fizzy water for days and days? When I finally got to a hotel room where I could turn on the tap and drink the water, what do you think I did? What would you do? I expect you, too, might gulp down nine glasses of water. But in that moment I began to thank God for tap water. And I began to realize why some people, like Charles, are serious when they talk to God about simple things.

Charles also told us how he prayed for airline pilots, not primarily that they would get him to his destination on time but that they would sense the wonderful peace of Christ in their lives and that they might enjoy their work of serving others as they were flying in God's beautiful heavens. He prayed earnestly for the attendants who rushed up and down the aisles that God would give them strength and courage to face angry, fearful, and disgruntled people, and that in the wisdom which comes from God they might sense in these people, in spite of their anxieties and tensions, that they also are indeed creatures of our God. To see people with the eyes of Christ ought to be the goal of every Christian. Have you discovered that secret?

And Charles loved the community of faith. The love of the community is not something merely to talk about. It is one of God's most marvelous gifts. When one senses love, one doesn't have to talk piously about it. As we seminary professors met year after year for prayer, exchanged our spiritual biographies, grew to understand one another in Christ in spite of the fact that we were Lutheran and Nazarenes, Presbyterians and Methodists, Episcopalians and Brethren, Baptists and many other types, we began to learn in a new way the meaning of risking community in Christ.

When we have thus prayed with others for years, heard their cries and concerns before God, listened to their innermost thoughts with the Almighty, we will not soon regard them as our enemies. To know someone in Christ Jesus is to discover the power of God in building community. I know that I will always be a staunch Baptist. My Baptist heritage is settled in my bones. My grandfathers and great-grandfathers were persecuted in Europe for being Baptists and I will not soon reject my heritage as a Baptist. I am a Baptist by conviction, but my heritage as a brother in Christ far surpasses my heritage as a Baptist. In Christ Jesus we need to learn how to risk community with one another even though we do not look alike or dress alike, speak the same languages, have the same accents, come from the same economic levels, support the same political parties, or are of the same sex. We need to risk community in Christ Jesus with those who are not like us because in so doing we learn something very important about God.

I suspect that by God's grace when we get to heaven we will be in for some mighty strange surprises. We may discover that God has a sense of humor. We may be seated at the great supper of the Lamb surrounded by those sons and daughters of God with whom we had the most disagreements. In heaven there will be no corners where likeminded people will be able to caucus together. So maybe it is time for us to learn what it means to risk community in love rather than merely talk about it.

Risking Community

Think for a moment about our usual patterns of taking sides on issues. Then reflect on the story of a former professor, Dr. Otto Piper of Princeton. During the second World War he was forced by Hitler to leave Germany in one day, and he ended up with one son in the German forces and one son in the American forces. As he spoke of that situation, he used to say "I learned something about war" and about "God as a parent who has children on both sides of almost every issue." "I loved my sons," said Dr. Piper, "and it was hard to lose them to the hellish struggles of humanity." Christians are called to be god-like in the midst of human arrogance. This lesson is not easy to learn.

We are called not to fear the insanities of the world but to risk love that builds community. This living of love—not talking about it—is the genuine key to identifying a Christian because, Jesus said, by this love "all people would know that you are my disciples" (John 13:35). Moreover, Christians need to learn personally the power that is inherent in love because "perfect (or authentic) love expels fear" (1 John 4:18).

Christians who seek honestly to live in the way of love discover a new sense of inner power that comes as a gift from God's very own presence in their lives. They are God's people who really struggle to risk love in community. They are the people who truly abide in Christ and find the joy which Jesus promised (John 15:11). They are the people of the new commandment because they have learned to love one another as Christ loved them (v. 12).

Risking community can be traumatic for some Christians. Those who either avoid others or exploit others in the name of Christ will find that risking community will be difficult. Both avoiders and exploiters will likely know intellectually the need for genuine love, but both will doubtless fear risking love because it means a real inability to control the situation.

Love, however, means treating other humans as genuine equals. To love someone else means giving up trying to control them. It means allowing God to deal with them. Indeed, it means allowing God to deal with you and your insecurities. Love means to trust that God is in your situation and that God is not insecure. God can deal in love with you and with others that are related to you. Love does not mean giving up your concerns. Love means giving your concerns about yourself and others to God. Risking community in Christ is what Jesus wants for all of the people of God. Will you begin today to risk anew the experience of community? You may discover that all you have to lose is fear!

9

The Courage to Risk Freedom in the Spirit

Rigidity and Group Fear

Now that you can see yourself within the story of the family of God, you come to one more major hurdle on the road to freedom from fear. That hurdle is the fearfulness of whole groups of people to risk living in the freedom of the Spirit. Group fear thrives in religion that is based on rules and warnings, under the eye of a stern, cruel, and punishing God. Signs of fear-ridden religion are the refusal to let people think for themselves; distrust of doubt even when doubts are clearly breaking up childish and magical thinking in search of deeper levels of faith; the demand that everyone conform to a rigid understanding of doctrine and to use only the "in" words to speak about their faith.

Should you find yourself in a faith group in which your fears are constantly stimulated, in which a harsh and critical spirit prevails, in which you are being pressed into conformity of behavior and of thought, you face another fearful choice. You must decide whether to allow yourself to be captured by the spirit of fear that surrounds you or to trust the spiritual freedom that you knew in your initial surrender to God. In this chapter, we want to help you explore these options and decide for yourself which way you will go as you continue your spiritual journey. You may be standing now on the brink of the freedom that will bring you out of your personal "land of bondage" and into the "Promised Land"—the land of obedience to the Spirit of God, the land of freedom from the intimidation and enslavement of a fear-ridden, legalistic community.

Christian Freedom and Galatians

Perhaps no book of the Bible spells out better the way that Christians need to deal with the subject of freedom than Paul's Letter to the Galatians. Martin Luther called this book the Magna Carta of Christian freedom! Every Christian needs to face honestly the impact of this book because, when Paul wrote to the Galatians, he was confronting a problem that has literally devastated the church and robbed Christians of the power of the Holy Spirit in their lives throughout the centuries.

The problem of the Galatian Christians was the problem of legalism. It was a problem in which the Galatians were adding strict rules and regulations to the salvation which is given in Christ Jesus. The proclaimers of this legalism were dictatorial Judaizers who were convinced that freedom in Christ needed to be strictly controlled by their statements of dos and don'ts which they derived from the Old Testament law. Moreover, these Judaizers insisted that—since circumcision was part of the Old Testament means of being identified as a member of God's people and "God didn't change his mind," then—this rite also applied to Christians.

These false proclaimers preyed on the insecurity of new Christians and loaded on the Gentiles the incredible burden of the Jewish law. By using this type of religious pattern, the Judaizers knew they could exert authority over the new converts and gain control over them. But Paul was not ready to let that happen. He had been an obedient, legalistic Jew. He had been a super Jew (compare Phil. 3:1-11). Judaism, however, was not Christianity. He discovered that legalism and Christian freedom sprang from two very different approaches to God. When Paul became a Christian, he gave up legalism and he was not prepared to sacrifice Christianity to any legalism thereafter.

So angry was he with these legalists that he really wished they would castrate themselves in their goal to circumcise the community. (See Gal. 5:12. Most translations are so mild that they lose the power of Paul's admonition!)

Legalism in any form is not Christianity. Paul knew that legalism was a human construction which sprang from humanity's desire to define the relationship to God in terms of human rules. Rules by definition are usually attainable, at least by some. But Paul knew that persons could not attain a right relationship with God on their own. Relationship with God could not be earned. It was a gift in Christ Jesus our Lord.

Therefore, Paul's judgment on preachers of legalism was *anathema* (the ultimate curse), even if those preachers of legalism would be angels from heaven (Gal. 1:8)! Martin Luther grasped the meaning of Paul and added that even though the preachers of legalism might be popes, they would be cursed! Today, to be fair, we must add that the curse applies even if those preachers and teachers are leaders of great denominations. Legalism and Christian freedom have been born out of two very different wombs. Legalism is a construct of humanity. Salvation and Christian freedom are the gift of God!

To emphasize the contrast, Paul asked the deceived Galatians if they actually thought that the presence of the Holy Spirit in their lives sprang from legalism (3:1-2). Moreover, he called them to ponder whether or not they had begun their Christian lives with the Holy Spirit and thereafter were trying to live out their lives as legalistic people of the flesh. If they were trying to do so, they needed to understand that their experience of salvation was really just an empty *(eikēi)* experience (vv. 3-4).

Legalism is a way of death. It is a way of the curse (v. 10). But faith is a way of life (v. 11). If legalism has any value, then its value is that it points us to hopelessness and to the necessity of Christ. It is a temporary measure, a *paidagōgos* (a substitute teacher, v. 24). It is, of course, better than no guidance. But it reveals to you your inabilities to attain perfection and therefore reveals to you your need for Christ. But as a Christian you must learn to live beyond the tortures of a legalistic life-style. Legalism is not your answer. It is bondage. Your life is to be lived under the marvelous direction of the Spirit which pulsated in Christ Jesus your Lord.

Christ has set you free to follow Him and not to become a slave of legalism (Gal. 5:1). But freedom in Christ does not mean that you have no guidance. Your task as a Christian is to reject fearful obedience to the dictators of the law and walk (conduct your life) according to the leading of the Spirit (v. 16). To walk with the Spirit is to reject all forms of impurity, sexual license, self-seeking, and rowdiness, and to bring forth attitudes and actions that truly represent the attributes of the Spirit like love, joy, peacefulness, patience, and all of the other qualities which are appropriate for the Christian (vv. 18-23). The model of what it means to be a Christian is not a set of rules but a Person. The only person who is worthy of being the Christian's model is Jesus Christ—the one who died and rose again for us (v. 24).

The Detour into Legalism

The lesson of Galatians shapes many of the great stories of the spiritual journey. John Bunyan, in his classic story of the Christian life, *The Pilgrim's Progress*, pictures legalism as a dangerous detour occurring quite early on the journey. Pilgrim had fled the City of Destruction, believing the warning of Evangelist and the words of Holy Scripture. With his head in the clouds and full of dreams of an easy walk to the Celestial City, Pilgrim fell into the Slough of Despond. The heavy burden on his back caused him to sink deeper and deeper into the mucky swamp until a helper pulled him out. Once more Evangelist came to him and pointed the way toward the Gate through which he must pass if he is to make progress on the spiritual journey.

Next, before reaching the Gate, Pilgrim was lured by Worldly Wiseman to take a detour into legalism. He headed off down a side road toward the Village of Morality to find a man named Mr. Legality who was supposed to be able to rid him of his burden at once. No sooner did Pilgrim come within sight of the legalistic haven than he found himself under the shadow of the dark mountain of Sinai—the source of "The Law," and the Old Testament authority to which Christians generally appeal in justifying a fear-ridden, legalistic religion. Suddenly Mount Sinai became a volcano, belching molten ash and poisonous gases. Pilgrim was terrified. Evangelist appeared again, this time delivering a stern warning against Pilgrim's choice of a quick fix for his problem of the burden of sin. But mercy shined through Evangelist's words of judgment and, once again, Pilgrim was shown the way toward the Gate through which he now passed safely on his way toward the Celestial City.

Bunyan saw legalism in religion as a danger to the life of the Spirit and, at best, as a delaying detour on the way toward wholehearted surrender to the Spirit of God. Pilgrim did not receive a transforming experience of Grace until he came to the Cross, and he could never have come to the Cross without passing through the Gate. At the cross the burden fell off by itself, rolled down the hill, and into the tomb where Jesus was buried and from which He rose from the grave. This was the first of many glad moments of perfect freedom in the Spirit. Never could Pilgrim have found the freedom to walk in the Spirit had he not been warned away from Mr. Legality and been encouraged to bear his heavy inner burden until the morning of spiritual awakening dawned. Like Evangelist in *The Pilgrim's Progress*, we offer this chapter as both a warning and a promise: a warning against the seduction of legalism as a quick fix for your inner pain and fears, and the promise of a better way—the way of walking in the freedom in the Spirit.

The Error of Legalism

Have you asked yourself why the high priests and the Pharisees received the most scathing attacks from the Lord Jesus? The cruel Romans were not treated nearly as harshly by Jesus as these Jews because Jesus recognized that the Jewish leadership in His day represented themselves as righteous in the presence of Yahweh, the God of Israel; but they failed to live by the pattern of God. Therefore, they were judged severely. In this respect, notice that in the conversation with Pilate, Jesus said "the one who handed me over to you has the more monstrous sin" (John 19:11).*

Who handed Jesus to Pilate? Of course, Judas betrayed Jesus, but not to Pilate. In the mind of John, the only one it could be was the high priest, the chief representative of God among the Jews. But in that day there were really two high priests. Caiaphas was the figurehead, but Annas never gave up his power, and he ran the show through his family. It was Annas combined with Caiaphas, therefore, who ultimately committed the greatest blasphemy when the high priests together apparently shouted, "We have no king but Caesar!" (John 19:15). The Old Testament can be written from the time of Samuel onward as the sad struggle of who would be recognized as the king of Israel (1 Sam. 8:7). Was their king to be God or was it to be a human appointee? Here in the time of Jesus, the chief priests committed the ultimate apostasy as they epitomized the lowest point of the struggle in Israel's history when they said, "We have no king but a Roman monarch!" The blasphemy was complete.

Both these high priests who represented the Sadducees, and their hostile counterparts, the Pharisees, had neatly packaged the faith of Israel. The poor people of Israel who were the subject of these prepackaged forms of faith were, from Jesus' viewpoint, like helpless sheep without a shepherd (Matt. 9:36). Israel's earthly shepherds in Jesus' day had clearly fulfilled the sad prophecies of Ezekiel 34. These representative shepherds were greedy and self-centered and they forced harsh rules on the people (compare vv. 3-4). True shepherds, however, were to love the crippled and the hurt because true shepherds were to be authentic representatives of none other than the Great Shepherd, God Himself (vv. 15-16). When Jesus came, He took the prophetic designation of the Good Shepherd very seriously and both modeled the correct spirit of the shepherd and scathingly condemned the hirelings (the leaders of the people) who failed to love the sheep as God expected them to do (see John 10).

The leaders of the people had placed a heavy yoke of rules upon the people and had threatened them with Divine judgment if they failed to follow their dictates. To point out the failure of the Jewish religious leaders of Jesus' day is not to be mistaken for being against all Jews. We must remember that the first members of the church were Jewish believers in Christ. Even though their religious leaders rejected Jesus, many Jews accepted Jesus as Messiah, Savior, and Lord.

By contrast, Jesus informed the people that His yoke was easy and His burden was light. He lovingly invited all who were burdened, who were like helpless babes, to take His yoke and learn from Him the genuine requirements of God (Matt. 11:25-30). Christ wants His people to be happy in following Him. He does not want pain to come to them as the result of trying to be obedient to some external set of rules. Christ's commands are not harsh rules but are built on loving God (John 14:15-21). If pain is to result from being a Christian, it is not to arise from God giving people rigid standards of life. Pain, of course, could be expected from other people who hate God's living standards and terrorize or persecute others who have discovered the joyful freedom of being in Christ. People who still need rules to find some form of personal acceptance generally cannot tolerate Christians who have found Christ's joyful freedom (15:18 to 16:4,32-33). Therefore, they seek to make others conform to their set of rules so that they can feel comfortable with those rules. For a Christian to give in to such rules of the legalists is to sell one's soul for acceptance in a fruitless legalistic community. Such a community stands condemned by God and, no matter how large or powerful it becomes, it is doomed by its own idolatry.

The Story of "The Dun Horse"

When the leaders of a community are driven by a spirit of fear and when they inspire a legalistic spirit in the whole community, those who want to stand fast in the freedom to which they were called will be pushed out to the margins of the group. Some people find it so hard to take the cool and critical treatment of the majority that they give up their spiritual freedom and "submit again to a yoke of slavery" (Gal. 5:1). Others become so hurt and angry that they defy the legalists who control the community. They tend, in Paul's words, to use their freedom "as an opportunity for the flesh." But there is another way, and that is "through love [to] be servants of one another (vv. 13). It is the way of walking in the Spirit (v. 16).

To walk by the Spirit is to shift your obedience from the harsh voices of those who are trying to live by the letter of the law to the "still, small voice" of the Spirit of God—the voice that you hear in your inmost self, the voice that nurtures you in the fruit of the Spirit—"love, joy, peace, patience, kindness, goodness, faithfulness, gentleness, self-control" (vv. 22-23).

You need not abandon your community of faith in anger. You may simply accept your place on the margins of the group for the time being and keep on listening for the voice of the Spirit who will use your faithfulness to bless the entire community in due time. The pressure to conform to the spirit of the group can be intense. The temptation to stop listening to the Spirit of God is great whether the majority are legalistic or whether they are merely advocating respectability" in religion. In either case you can expect to be pushed out to the margin of the majority. Living in obedience to the voice of the Spirit when the majority are full of pride and self-righteousness or "strife" and "party spirit" (v. 20) is the theme of an old, old story of the Pawnee Indians: "The Story of the Dun Horse." (Dun is the color of the horse: a dull grayish brown.) Here is a condensed version of the story:

Many years ago, an old Pawnee woman lived with her sixteen-year-old grandson. They had no relations and were so poor that they were despised by the rest of the tribe. One day the boy stumbled upon a miserable, old, worn-out dun horse. The old woman and her boy claimed the horse as their own. They loved it and provided for it as best they could.

One day the young braves raced back to camp to tell the chiefs of a large herd of buffalo nearby among which was a spotted calf. Now for the Pawnee, a spotted robe is *ti-war-uks-ti:* big medicine. So the head chief announced that the young man who killed the spotted calf would have his beautiful daughter for his wife.

On the day of the big hunt, the rich braves on their fast horses laughed at the poor boy and his dun horse, but an amazing thing happened. Suddenly the horse turned his head round and spoke to the boy. He told the boy just what to do, and when the hunt began the dun horse seemed to sail along like a bird. Well, in no time at all, the poor boy's arrow felled the spotted calf. All the others were amazed to see that the old dun horse had changed. The boy brought a great load of meat home to his grandmother and gave her the spotted skin for a robe. The old woman laughed, for her heart was glad.

That night the horse spoke again to the boy, telling him that a large war party of the Sioux was coming to attack the village the next day. He told the boy that he was to make four charges into the middle of the Sioux and was to kill their head chief and three more of their bravest warriors. "But," the horse added, "don't go again. If you go the fifth time, maybe you will be killed, or else you will lose me. Remember." And the boy promised.

The next day everything happened just as the horse had said. The poor boy killed the head chief and three of the bravest Sioux without getting a scratch. But the fighting continued. After standing around and watching the battle for awhile, the boy decided to mount his horse and charge into the battle again. No more was he among the Sioux than an arrow struck his horse dead. The boy fought his way through the Sioux and ran for dear life back to the Pawnees. But the Sioux took their knives and hatchets and cut the horse up into small pieces.

At nightfall, the boy went outside the village to a hilltop to mourn the loss of his horse. A great windstorm came up, and after the wind a rain. Through the rain, the boy could just see the pile of flesh and bones which was all that was left of his horse. His heart was heavy and he kept on mourning.

Storm after storm raged through the night. As the light dawned the poor boy saw the most amazing thing of all. His old dun horse rose up and looked around. The boy raced down the hill to his horse. As soon as he was near, the horse spoke saying, "You have seen how it has been this day; and from this you may know how it will be after this. But *Ti-ra-wa* [The Great Spirit] has been good, and has let me come back to you. After this, do what I tell you; not any more, not any less!" And from that time on the boy did as he was told.

The story of "The Dun Horse" ends in these words: Now the boy was rich, and he married the beautiful daughter of the head chief, and when he became older, he was made head chief himself. He had many children by his beautiful wife. He always took good care of his old grandmother, and kept her in his own lodge until she died. The dun horse was never ridden except at feasts, and when they were going to have a doctors' dance, but he was always led about with the chief, wherever he went. The horse lived in the village for many years, until he became very old and died.[1]

The Parable of the Dun Horse Interpreted

While the story of the dun horse may seem strange to people who think about rockets and microchips, it reminds us of something that is true in every age: *the secret of living well no matter how bad your external circumstances is to love and to trust the voice of the Spirit of God.*

The poor boy and his grandmother were living on the margin of a community that treated them harshly. They were not expelled from the community, but they were never allowed to forget that they were not really *in* the community either. Finding the dun horse did not help them find acceptance. But, unknown to anyone, the dun horse is, in reality, an incarnation of The Great Spirit. The poor boy and his grandmother had found the greatest of treasures in the old, ugly, worn-out horse. Although they did not know the horse's value, they loved it and they took care of it in spite of their poverty. No one in the community saw the real value of the dun horse, either. They were blind to The Great Spirit living in horse flesh among them.

Native Americans in the old days believed in a God of love, and even though they had not heard of the incarnation of God in human flesh, they believed that God took form in animals and birds in order to speak with human beings, to help and to heal them in times of trouble.

The great surprise in the story is that the dun horse spoke to the boy. The boy was afraid and his fear tells us that he knew he was in the presence of The Great Spirit. Then in the hunt for the spotted calf, the whole tribe received the revelation: the dun horse was The Great Spirit in their midst! Seeing the miracle before their eyes must have shaken the tribe to its very roots. Here was The Great Spirit in the form of an old, ugly, worn-out, and perfectly miserable horse. It was living at the edge of the camp, despised by all, and being cared for only by the poorest and least important people of the tribe. All of a sudden, the power of the chiefs in the tribe, their fine horses and beautiful wives and children, meant nothing in comparison to the poor boy's dun horse. He, the boy they had mocked and despised, was now the truly great one, the one who would marry the head chief's daughter and become the greatest of all.

Surprises like this happen all the time in people's lives. You can see such wonders if you open your eyes to see the miracles that take place within the hearts of people. A person may drive hard to be among the bright and beautiful people of a community, to have a share in the power, and to rule over others. Lacking real power, such a person often will lord it over the weak and poor in the group. Now look within yourself and see if a similar thing may be happening. You force yourself to fit the expectations of the community of people that matters most to you. You push off to the margins of your awareness the weak and the poorly developed aspects of your inner self. All too often what gets cut out is a person's capacity for love and loyalty toward the poor and the weak, the old and those who are no longer good for heavy work or for fighting battles that are important to you. Then a crisis may come, a coveted prize may be lost, the values by which you have lived your life may begin to crumble underfoot. Then you begin to see clearly that the true meaning of life is in love and loyalty to the Spirit of Love and Truth which you previously pushed aside. At such a moment your heart will be divided between hating what you now know to be truly important and secretly envying what you have neglected in your own spiritual journey. The stage is set for a terrible internal battle. But that is getting ahead of the story a bit.

The spotted calf was the first prize that the dun horse enabled the poor boy to win. To the Pawnees a spotted calf meant hope for healing and well-being and a place of honor in the community. It is when your longings for healing within your self are awakened that you are most ready to open your eyes and see the true source of healing. In killing the spotted calf, the boy discovered that the power to claim healing and blessing from the whole community was within his reach. Its source was The Great Spirit. Although he may not have fully realized it, the power was made available to him because he had not become bitter and self-pitying in being pushed off to the margin of the tribe. Instead, he had loved and cared for a miserable creature just as it was. In fact, without realizing it, he had nurtured The Great Spirit within himself. Nothing was more important to him. As the dun horse was his closet companion, so The Great Spirit was within him. Both the horse and the boy were despised by others, but the boy's spirit of love for the weak ones of the world was proof that he had chosen the better part. Without knowing, he had befriended The Great Spirit and in due time The Great Spirit came shining through the veil of flesh, bringing blessing not only to the boy but to the whole community as well.

Immediately after The Great Spirit was revealed to the community, a great battle broke out. Is this not true to much of life? No sooner does a person have a peak experience of the Presence of God than battles break out all over. Of course there is the inner battle of doubts and fears. Sometimes this battle spreads to family and friends who tell you that you are crazy to take a spiritual experience so seriously. They may dismiss you as being weird. At other times the battle may spread into a whole community. When a religious denomination or a nation or any other in-group is faced with the reality that the Spirit of Truth is not in the old ways or the old words alone, when the Spirit of God is clearly working in those who were formerly despised, a frightening conflict may be set off.

The voice of The Great Spirit guided the poor boy to the spotted hide for healing and to the blessing of the community in the buffalo hunt. Then the dun horse spoke again to guide the boy through the dangers of battle. The voice of The Great Spirit told the boy to charge into battle four times—no more and no less. The boy promised but, inflated with his success and a new sense of power, he broke his promise and charged a fifth time. His horse was killed and he barely got out alive.

Once more the story of the dun horse becomes a parable of the spiritual journey. As soon as you learn to listen and to hear the voice of the Spirit, you can count on receiving wise guidance through the dangers that beset you. You will be able to move with a courage and confidence that you never knew before. You may expect to win battles and earn the praise and honor of your community. But then things may go wrong.

It often takes a bitter experience to learn to respect the inner voice. For the poor boy it seemed that everything was lost. Out on the hilltop the night after the battle, alone, deep in his grief, he looked down on the battlefield and saw nothing but a pile of flesh and bones where once the dun horse had carried him to triumph after triumph. Terrible storms of wind and rain beat against the scene, wave after wave. The storms fit the inner reality of the boy who was torn with guilt, grief, hopelessness, and fear for the future. It was indeed a dark night of the soul.

In the darkness and the storms something began to move. The pieces of the dun horse began to come together again. Then, marvel of marvels, the dun horse was standing up— alive! The boy ran to the horse, embraced it, and without a spoken word he committed himself wholeheartedly to absolute

THE CRISIS OF FEAR

obedience to the voice of The Great Spirit. He then became a chief—ruler over his own spirit in obedience to the Spirit of God. He was linked in marriage to the head chief. He became a wise and caring person for the whole community, and most certainly for his elderly grandmother and for the dun horse.

The story of the dun horse has a happy ending not because life is free of problems once a person learns to trust and to obey the voice of the Spirit, but because the companionship of the Spirit carries with it true inner freedom no matter how rejecting a person's community may have been.

Jesus responded to the rejection of the cities "where most of his mighty works had been done" with words of warning. But then He turned to God in a prayer of gratitude that while the "wise and understanding" had rejected Him, God had "revealed" His Presence "to babes." It is almost as though Jesus were the Great Dun Horse of His day. As such, His true identity was revealed to those who were forced to live on the margins of the tribe, scorned by the "wise and understanding."

Guidance from 1 John

The First Epistle of John has provided Christians with an important word of guidance in the midst of conflicting demands arising within a community. Not every spirit within the church is from God. Therefore, Christians need to test the spirits to determine whether they are really from Christ or are the result of an "antichrist" spirit in the church (1 John 41-3). Confessing Jesus does not merely mean saying His name or reciting some doctrines of the church. It means authentically listening to God and hearing His voice (v. 6). When a person really hears God, that person will know the difference between the spirit of truth and the spirit of falsehood (v. 6). Notice that the emphasis falls on the two different spirits in the community. To listen to the spirit of truth means that fear is banished because God who is *in us* is greater than the spirit that is in the world (v. 4).

A second word of guidance is also given by John in this same context. It is a word that involves a person's basic motivation toward others and it is exemplified in a person's style of life. You can tell an authentic Christian and an authentic Christian community by love.

Love is the means for overcoming fear (v. 18). Christians love because Christ has first loved them (v. 19). If anyone is filled with words about loving God or fellow Christians but does not evidence such love in the way he or she acts toward others then John is clear about what God's judgment is: such a person is a liar (v. 20)! Moreover, a verbal nonloving community is merely a shell of a church and we as Christians need to understand such a reality. Love in the community is not a matter of words; it is a matter of loving action. The way of love in the community is the only sure foundation for dealing with the fears that arise from pseudo-Christian patterns in the church (v. 18). True love is born from God, because "God is love" (v. 8). True love gives confidence to Christians in the face of opposition (v. 17) and it motivates Christians to begin to live in the perfect manner of Christ, their Lord (v. 12).

Our concern in writing this chapter is to assist those who have confessed Christ as their Savior to learn to discern the spirits that confront them within the community. The Bible teaches us not to fear but to discern both the spirits that ought to be within a Christian community and those that are typically present in the world. We certainly need to know *what* we believe because the spirit of falseness is abroad in the world and it confronts Christians even in their communities of faith (1 John 3:5-6). But we also need to embody God's Spirit in our living because *how* we believe and act is even more important. To exhibit unloving belief is to live the life of hypocrisy which Jesus fiercely condemned (Matt. 23) and which Paul called an empty sham (1 Cor. 13:1-2).

The Jewish leadership in Jesus' day made the test of *what* people believed the mark of membership. In their fanatical quest to obey what they thought was God's will, they killed the Lord Jesus, God's unique messenger, and they stoned and persecuted His followers. They prized purity of doctrine, but sacrificed purity of heart. That split is not the way of God. Purity of doctrine alone births hatred and fear. It does *not* bring forth love and confidence in God. It is not the way of Christ and the gospel. Jesus modeled instead the life-giving way that creates community. In His life He faced the possible extinction of both His life and His goal of the new community. But the enemies and manipulators of love forgot then and continue to forget today that there is still a God at work in the world!

Should we then fear for Christ's cause? Did He fear for it? Did He fight for it? He chose the cross, knowing that to respond to His enemies with fear and hate would be to destroy not only His enemies but also His cause. He suffered and died not only because of *what* He believed, but also because of *how* He believed—because He believed with suffering love.[2]

We have written much in recent chapters about courage: the courage to believe in the terrifying God, the courage to die to fear and be reborn, the courage to risk community, and now, the courage to risk freedom in the Spirit. Beyond courage, however, is love. True courage is rooted in love. The courage that it takes to overcome a lifetime of deep-seated fears is not bootstrap courage. It cannot be pulled out of yourself alone. The courage which overcomes springs spontaneously out of your willingness to be loved by God. It is not merely a way of thinking. It is a way of allowing yourself to be loved. It is a way of walking in the freedom of the Spirit and allowing the Spirit, who is perfect Love, to cast out fear. Overcoming courage is, in a word, fearless love. God invites you—and all of us—to live with fearless love. In our final chapter, therefore, we turn to the theme of living with fearless love in church and society.

Part IV
Conclusion

10
Fearless Love in Church and Society

Impelled by Love

To live with fearless love in the church and in society requires a sense of confidence that does not come from any mere human resource. We have been talking at length in these chapters about such confidence. It is rooted in something far different than a do-it-yourself Christianity. It is a way of life that finds its strength beyond oneself.

That something, that strength that comes from "beyond," is a relationship with God as perfect Love. In such a relationship you share the "great flash of understanding" that came to Dante at the end of his journey into the presence of the living God: " . . . like a wheel in perfect balance turning, I felt my will and my desire impelled by the Love that moves the sun and the other stars."[1]

God's perfect love healed the pilgrim's inner conflicts between the will pushing in one way and the desire for God pulling in another. He found wholeness and freedom from fear as both will and desire were "impelled" by the Love that moves the whole universe. And it is so, not just in story but also in everyday living!

Furthermore, Dante's vision of God is also a vision of your own true self. The God manifest in nature, revealed in Jesus Christ, and ever present in the Holy Spirit is, *whether you are aware of it or not,* your very energy for living. As surely as the sun runs its course and the stars send out their awesome sparks from millions of light years away, so surely you are made alive by the One who is perfect Love. Let your eyes be opened and you will see the Source of wholeness, inner harmony, and the power of fearless love at work in the core of your own inmost self, as well as in the entire universe. For to see God is to see perfect Love. To experience perfect Love is to be empowered with a truly fearless love. Once you begin to experience fearless love, you know that only the fear of the Lord sets you free from fear.

This is the message that the New Testament writers proclaimed about fear and fearlessness. Nowhere is the message more clearly developed than in the First Epistle of Peter.

Impelled by Love: A Model from 1 Peter

As Peter wrote this letter, he knew that the little communities of Christians in Asia Minor had many reasons to feel almost overwhelmed by the power structures of their day. Therefore, he did not address them as powerful leaders in society. Instead, he chose to refer to them as "exiles" or "aliens" *(parepidēmois)*, people who seemed out of place, whose home was really somewhere else (1 Pet. 1:1). But, at the same time as he called them aliens, he reminded them that they were especially selected and destined by God for a wonderful life of obedience in Christ Jesus (vv. 1-2).

In this forceful letter Peter restated for all Christians the idea that their citizenship rights were with God and that their expected inheritance was built upon the great Christian confession of Jesus Christ's resurrection (v. 3). Their hope, therefore, would never rust or rot like things do. It would never be polluted or defiled like water and wealth can become. And it would never vanish or fade like dreams and expectations often do. The Christian's hope is firmly established in heaven and thoroughly protected by God (vv. 4-5).

The question then is how are Christians to live? Peter was

emphatic that Christians ought to live with *only one fear*, the fear of God (v. 17; 2:17)! But this fear of God is not a terrorizing fear. Instead, Peter told Christians to cast all their worries or concerns or fears upon God "because he cares" for them (5:7). God loves His people and wants the best for them. He wants to protect them from everything that would harm them (vv. 8-10).

The fear of God then is a recognition that God is not controlled by human manipulation. God is in a category apart. You cannot put God in a test tube and you cannot use God for your own purposes. You may attempt to use the church or any other institution or person in society for your own ends. But you will never use God in that way. The truth is that God ought to be using you and your task as a Christian is to discover how God desires to use you.

Peter charged Christians to be holy or pure and to conduct their lives as obedient people (1:15-22). But the manner of their living or the characteristic pattern that is to mark their lives is love (v. 22). This love, however, is not based on fear. It is a love that becomes fearless because Christians have been born of God and God lives in them (v. 23). The Christian's responsibility then is to grow up and model the meaning of living with God. It is to put behind or reject all patterns of life that are inappropriate for Christians (2:1-2). Because Christians are the people of God (vv. 9-10) they are to live before others as examples of integrity (vv. 11-12).

The Christian's greatest example is none other than Jesus, the suffering Shepherd, who modeled sinless strength in His death. He, therefore, challenges all Christians "to follow in his tracks" of fearless, self-giving love (vv. 21-25).* This fearless love is epitomized in the spirit of servanthood and Peter expected Christians to evidence such fearless love in all relationships of life. This self-giving servanthood pertains to the context of the state (vv. 13-16), to the workplace (vv. 18-20), to the home (3:1-7) and particularly to the Christian community (5:1-6). It is a pattern of life that represents authentic Christianity.

Moreover, those who take the name of Christ should not be surprised by the presence of pain and suffering in their lives. Suffering was clearly evident in the life of Jesus, and Peter had little doubt that it would be part of his readers' experience as well. Therefore, believers should not think it strange if suffering and even persecution were to come their way (4:12). To be hated for the name of Christ can prove the integrity or genuineness of a person's faith (1:6). The worst the world can do is end the Christian's physical life. But this realization also means that at such a point the Christian does not have to be concerned with sin any more (4:1). Peter's concern, however, was that if the Christian suffers, it must never be because the Christian has acted in a destructive, hateful, hurtful, or immoral manner (v. 15).

You as a Christian are to shun the unethical and immoral patterns of the world and you are not to fear or worry about the powerful forces in the world. If the world returns to you pain and persecution for fearless love, you are to rejoice because, as Peter said, you are then able to participate more fully in the sufferings of Christ (v. 13). These words are really shocking in their implications for most of us and this style of life is not easy to accept. It is not the message of many popular media preachers who promise easy success to Christians. But it is the way of fearless love that is proclaimed in the Bible. It is the overcoming pattern which enables you to entrust your very life to the one who first created you (v. 19) and birthed you anew in Christ Jesus (1:3-9).

Suffering is a pattern of life that is not talked about very much in twentieth-century Western Christianity and, as a result, pain is something many Christians do not handle very well. But fearless love is rooted in a firm conviction that meaning is not derived from the patterns and successes of this world. Fearless love is founded upon a confidence in God who provides meaning to life and makes sense out of the senselessness in the world. To fear God, then, is not only the beginning of wisdom (Prov. 9:10), it is the source of genuine, fearless love. And fearless love is the authentic beginning of the end of fearful living.

To fear or not to fear, therefore, is *not* the great question of your life. The question instead is: who and what do you fear? To fear the self-giving loving and caring God who gives fearless confidence to life is the biblical and Christian way of dealing with fear.

Impelled to Care

Allow the fear of the loving God to drive out your old fearfulness about the dangers of everyday things and gradually you will find yourself impelled to move toward others who are cringing in fear before the darkness that surrounds them. You are impelled to care.

Among the great biblical example of a person who was deeply impelled to care for others stands the figure of Barnabas. Not only was he the one who searched for the transformed Saul when others might have been hesitant about fully accepting him (Acts 11:25), but Barnabas was also the one who gave Mark a second chance when Paul had firmly categorized him as a "quitter" (15:36-39). Think about the implications of giving a person a second chance. Remember this quitter was the man called Mark who later gave us what may have been the first full-scale Gospel! When Luke described the caring Barnabas he called him a "good man" who was "full of the Holy Spirit and faith" (11:24). What a magnificent description for any Christian!

But do you remember how he was introduced to readers? He was brought to our attention because the apostles gave him a special name: the son of support or help (*paraklēseōs*, 4:36), the same basic term in Greek that is used for the function of the Holy Spirit. He received this designation because he cared. Indeed, he sold his property and brought the money to the church in order to help the needy (v. 37).

But consider how different the situation was with Ananias and Sapphira (5:1-11). They, too, sold their property and gave some of the money to the church. Yet, they hardly received the blessing of the apostles or God. Instead, they tried to cheat the community by informing the apostles that they had turned all the proceeds over to the church. As a result, Peter was called upon to render the judgment of God for their deception and both of them died as the result of trying to lie to God (vv. 4-5, 9-10).

The issue here was not one of giving money to the church. Truly, in both cases the parties gave money to the Christian community. The issue was one of motive. How different was the motive of Ananias and Sapphira from that of Barnabas.

These contrasting stories then point to an extremely important distinction which we need to understand very clearly. Not all so-called acts of caring are really the same. Not all stem from the same motives and not all are impelled by unselfish love. There are many reasons why people are involved in caring for others. The question, therefore, must be asked: Why do you care?

Unhappily a great deal of care is given out of fearful love for others. Caring out of a sense of *duty* is one example. Duty may be heroically done, but duty always carries a bagful of rocks on its back. The rocks are fears of feeling guilty if the duty is not performed; fears of feeling resentful about having to be the one who is duty-bound. Duty may require you to put your dreams for yourself on hold—sometimes forever. Resentments, then, go hand in hand with self-pity. Often they turn into bitterness when others do not appreciate your sacrifices.

Dutiful caring may also be linked with the need to be cared for in return. Somehow it does not matter how much you do for others, you still may wonder who will be there to care for you when you need help. Knowing that the time will come when you will need to be cared for adds rocks to the bag of fear that you carry on your back.

The need for *approval* may drive you to care for others, but approval is never enough. You may gain a reputation as the most loving person around, but the need for approval will not let you rest. The voice of fear whispers in your inner ear: "But, if they really knew me, they wouldn't like me."

The need to *feel important,* to feel that you are making a difference in the lives of others, powers the drive in many to serve, to inspire, to invent better ways to do things. This drive, too, is often the result of a fearful love. For you can never be sure that your service will not be taken for granted. Who will remember? Will anyone give you credit for making a contribution to their life? What if, after all your caring, you are forgotten?

Another fearful love, one that is really hard to see in yourself, is caring for others to *avoid* paying attention to your own *pain.* Much of the glib advice that people give to one another is prompted by the need to avoid feeling the pain of another person. This is the reason why advice giving seldom helps anyone except the person who gives it. Even the advice givers receive little genuine comfort out of their advice. When advice giving is a shield against experiencing your own pain, you are never free of the fear that the shield will break down and leave you exposed to the raw pain of being just another vulnerable human being.

Fearful love, no matter how many forms it takes, does not compare with the fearless love born in a vision of the "Eternal Light." In writing of the experience of Inner Light, Thomas R. Kelly noted, "He plucks the world out of our hearts, loosening the chains of attachment. And He hurls the world into our hearts, where we and He together carry it in infinitely tender love."[2] To see God is to be "impelled" by Love into a double movement of the self: in Kelly's words again, "We must hasten unto God; and we must hasten into the world."[3] We are not "impelled" by a sense of duty, by pity, by self-serving motives of any kind when the vision of Love is fresh. Rather we are "impelled by the Love that moves the sun and the other stars." Once you are motivated by such Love, you discover that the power for life comes from beyond yourself. You know yourself to be moved by the energy of the universe, a willing spirit in the service of the Spirit of God—in and for the world.

In the Kew Gardens near London stands a magnificent gate to a Japanese temple—a gift from Japan to the British people. Facing the gate, as if to enter the temple, you see two lattice-type, brass-work sculptures. On the right is a warrior mounted on horseback, tightly holding the reins. He is clad in armor, sword at his side. He rides confidently—proud and self-important! On the left, as if leaving the temple, is the same person, stripped naked, clinging with bare hands and knees to the back of a sea serpent that is diving into the mysteries of the deep.

The gate tells a story like that which Dante tells. It is like the story that Thomas Kelly told and the lessons that the Holy Scriptures teach. It is the story of what happens when a person enters a place of worship and allows the vision to come. All the trappings of self-importance are stripped away; the tightly held reins by which a person hopes to stay in control are gone. For the high and mighty it is pride and pretension that are laid bare. For the low and weakly it is the excuses and the hiding places that are ripped away. Instead of the war-horse, there is a sea serpent (an Oriental symbol of the loving Deity) carrying the worshiper into depths not entered before, on a mission beyond the power of a person to control or fully to understand.

The sea serpent captures some of the meaning of being "impelled by the Love" that moves the universe. A person who has experienced God holds on for dear life while being carried by a Power that comes from beyond. It is this Power, the power of God moving in every atom and cell of the universe, the power of love revealed in Jesus Christ, that impels you to care, "to hasten into the world." Psychology describes the process by which a person faced with a threatening situation will respond with either fight or flight. In the Presence of "Eternal Light" you discover a third option: you are "impelled" to care in fearless love, riding bareback on the mighty, moving sea serpent into the depths of the Divine mystery at work in the world.

Impelled to Care: A Pauline Model

As one reads the fascinating stories of the apostle Paul one gains a little insight into the impelling force of love that must have driven the great missionary to the Gentiles. He and Barnabas, you remember, were called gods at Lystra after Paul healed a crippled man there. But the loyalty to Christ of these two Christian servants led them to refuse the accolades of the crowd. Instead of honor, therefore, by a strange twist of circumstances these two men were shortly thereafter nearly stoned to death by the same fickle crowd (Acts 14:8-19).

Yet, that pattern was not an isolated event in the life of Paul. Not long after, in the city of Philippi, Paul healed a possessed girl. But economic interests got in the way of the healing and Paul and Silas, after being beaten, were thrown into prison. Instead of whimpering about their imprisoned plight, however, they sang and prayed in jail and God used their Christian zeal and integrity to bless those around them, including the jailer himself (Acts 16:11-40). Praising God *in prison?* Do you not ask yourself: what kind of an internal working power held this man together when most people would fall apart?

And what was it in meeting with the Ephesian elders at Miletus that made Paul more interested in their plight than in his own well-being, especially since he obviously knew that he was headed to the beginning of his end at Jerusalem (Acts 20:17-38)? Why was he not afraid and why was he able to calm their troubled hearts with a word from Jesus that "it is more blessed to give than to receive" (v. 35)? What made a person like Paul tick?

Do you have such an impelling power in your own life? How do you measure yourself? Indeed, as you read of Paul's encounter with the Ephesian elders and then with the Christians at Caesarea (21:7-14) do you hear again the question "why are you weeping?" And what about Paul's answer: "I am ready not only to be shut away in prison but also to die . . . for . . . Jesus" (v. 13)? Does not your heart burn with a prayer like: *Oh, God give me a similar sense of your empowering presence and your overwhelming love that will banish fear from my life?* How like the Savior was this Paul who set his face like an arrow steadfastly to go to Jerusalem as the dark clouds of his destiny began to rise.

But there is one text in Paul that can cause even the best of Christian interpreters to cringe a little because of the power of its impact. In the ninth chapter of Romans, Paul made the startling announcement that he cared so much for his people who are lost without Christ that he would be willing to be cursed and chopped off from Christ if it would bring about their salvation (v. 3). What a model of self-giving love! Remember that the most important aspect of Paul's life was his hope in Christ. But he was so filled with loving anguish for others that he was willing to sacrifice himself for others. When you read Paul, therefore, do not fail to recognize such an all-encompassing sense of love in his life. To fail to understand this deep motivation in Paul is to fail to grasp who Paul really was.

Christ had made this self-centered religious bigot and persecutor into an incredible self-sacrificing servant. The caring for his little hurting flock is one of the most consistent patterns of Paul's writings. His caring is evidenced beautifully in the Thessalonian correspondence where he likens himself to a nurse who lovingly cares for infants or to a father who patiently encourages his children (1 Thess. 2:7-12). Yet Paul's parenting style was not without a backbone as he showed the rebellious Corinthians (1 Cor. 4:14-21; 3:1-3; 14:20). But the self-giving nature of his spirit is perhaps most clearly discernible in the later period of his ministry as Paul wrote to the Philippians. Here he modeled for all Christians how to deal with selfish rivalries among them (1:15-18). Moreover, he called them to accept suffering as a companion quality to believing (v. 29) and he reminded them that their model of Christian life is none other than the self-giving Jesus who willingly emptied Himself of majesty and adopted the fate of a crucified slave to provide for their salvation (2:5-11). This pattern Paul himself readily accepted (vv. 17-18) and summoned his children in the faith to imitate. Indeed, he directed them to follow other models who evidenced a similar self-giving commitment in their lives (3:18). Such is the Pauline model and imperative—a life impelled by self-giving love.

Impelled to See "What Is"

To be impelled by Love delivers you from the misery and the blindness of a divided and fearful heart, as we have seen. The experience of the Presence of the God, of perfect Love, unifies the heart. You discover the inner freedom to be wholehearted, not only about your personal goals and relationships, but also in your devotion to God and the care of your neighbors. Wholeheartedness is what the Beatitude is about when Jesus said, "Blessed are the pure in heart, for they shall see God" (Matt. 5:8). The readiness to *see* God is linked in surprising ways to being able to see "what is" in every area of life.

Has it occurred to you, for example, that when you are living with a divided heart in which you do not do what you want, but do the very things you hate (Rom. 7:15), that your basic problem may be one of *seeing?* And the problem is not one that an eye doctor can fix. The problem is one of spiritual seeing—seeing what is really going on at the level of your inner conflicts. For spiritual seeing includes seeing into your inmost spirit as well as seeing who God really is and what is possible in your relationship with God. Jesus put it this way: "if your eye is sound, your whole body will be full of light; but if your eye is not sound, your whole body will be full of darkness. If then the light in you is darkness, how great is the darkness!" (Matt. 6:22-23). In the everyday world the inability or unwillingness to see "what is" both blinds and destroys people. Indeed, the failure to see "what is" can destroy families, churches, and even nations.

The ancient story of Oedipus is about the fear of seeing what is really going on in a person's inner life, in a marriage and family, as well as in a whole society. Oedipus was the king of a Greek city state. A terrible plague had befallen the people. Oedipus sent to the oracle at Delphi and learned that the plague was a punishment upon the land because someone had killed his father and married his mother. The king then vowed to leave no stone unturned until the guilty person was found and punished.

As the story is told, the reader is made aware that Oedipus is, himself, the guilty one. For Oedipus was born to the former king and queen but exposed as an infant, because of his father's fear of being supplanted. Reared by a woodsman who found the infant, Oedipus unwittingly slayed his father and heroically saved the city state from a terrible danger. As a result, he was made the new king and given the old queen, his natural mother, as his wife.

Eventually Oedipus discovers the startling truth about himself: he has killed his father and married his mother and therefore his whole realm is sick with a plague. What does Oedipus do then? Instantly, he thrusts a poker into the fire until it is red hot and gouges out both of his eyes. For the rest of his life he is doomed to wander about the countryside as a blind man, attended only by one of his daughters.

Reflecting on the story, the tragedy of Oedipus is not that he was cast out as an infant, not that he unwittingly killed his father and married his mother. In these sad and horrible events Oedipus was the victim of cruelty and ignorance. His fate was the curse of the sins of the fathers upon succeeding generations. The tragedy of Oedipus is that when his search for the truth about his troubled life broke open before him, he crumbled and destroyed himself. He *chose* to blind himself rather than to see the truth, the "what is" about himself, his family, and his world.

Let us not be harsh in our judgment of Oedipus, however. We may find that we, ourselves, can be judged by the judgment we pass. Who of us does not bear the curse of our ancestors' ignorance, blind ambition, addictions, and/or cruelty? No matter how favored the conditions of a person's birth and rearing, who of us does not know the inner conflict and chaos of rage against a parent or the emotional pain or over-attachment, or both? And who of us cannot see, if we dare to look honestly, our own complexes, prejudices, hatreds, stupidities, lusts, ambitions, and fears magnified many times over in the conditions of our world? Out of our own inner chaos we unwittingly inflict plagues of pain and suffering on those around us. To some extent our entire world of influence suffers because of our unresolved conflicts.

Accordingly, the story of Oedipus is not just about a family in ancient times. It is the story of everyone—today and always. It is a story about the temptation to blind ourselves to the truth of "what is" in our lives rather than to face up to life with open eyes. Everyone makes life-changing choices when faced with the "what is" of one's own life. You may choose, for example, to blind yourself with addictions. An addiction is an addiction whether it involves the abuse of drugs and alcohol, the abuse of your own health in overwork, or the abuse of a spouse and children in promiscuity or sexual exploitation within the home. Alternately, you may blind yourself with fanatical resistance to change, you may give yourself over to be cruel, and even persecute those you judge to be evil. Or, again, you may let yourself be consumed by ambition that blinds you to the needs and rights of others. You also may blind yourself by hiding in the details of daily life. Indeed, you may live ever so respectably while choosing blind loyalty to traditional values and a blind faith in a primitive God. Blindness, in this sense can be just as sad and empty a way of life as was blind Oedipus who wandered through the second half of his life dependent upon the care of his daughter.

In the midst of so much meaninglessness in our world, the wonder is that many people have actually come to face the "what is" with open eyes, with courage and humility, with faith, hope, and love. The deepest dimension of the tragedy of Oedipus, however, is that he had never seen the great "what is" about God. He was his own god and a pitiful god at that. Oedipus's god had not suffered and died at the hands of evil people and their still more evil systems of religion and government. Oedipus's god could not accept or forgive a person trapped in the sins of the past and the meaningless tragedy of the present. Oedipus's god had not risen from the dead to become the Spirit of Comfort and a true Guide for all who believe. Oedipus's god was unable to transform a moment of seeing the "what is" about one's troubled life into a new birth as a child of the Almighty God who is perfect Love.

On the broader perspective it is also vital to recognize that the type of choices one makes about personal and family matters are similarly made by groups of people about their churches, political issues, and about national and international affairs. Groups, like individuals, decide whether to face the truth of "what is" or they blind themselves into believing that drifting with the currents of the culture will somehow turn out all right.

One of the most critical choices people make in the gathered community called Church is whether to maintain the unity of faith and love or to allow faith and love to be split apart. Every Christian knows that Jesus summed up all the Commandments in a single twofold imperative: "You shall love the Lord your God with all your heart, and with all your soul, and with all your mind. This is the great and first commandment. And a second is like it. You shall love your neighbor as yourself. On these two commandments depend all the law and the prophets" (Matt. 22:37-40).

When you understand the incredible significance of loving God with your whole being and your neighbor like yourself, you will begin to realize that every doctrine is to be weighed in the scale alongside of the great commandment. If the doctrine increases the love of God and neighbor, it is sound. If it contradicts the love of God and neighbor, it needs to be revised or rejected. Oscar Pfister put the matter in these words: "Whatever is irrelevant to love as understood by Jesus is also irrelevant to . . . faith."[4] Paul stated it even more forcefully: "And if I have prophetic powers, and understand all mysteries and all knowledge, and if I have all faith, so as to remove mountains, but have not love, I am nothing" (1 Cor. 13:2). The life of Jesus set the standard by which the church is to measure its life and its message. The dogmas and definitions of faith by which people try to force conformity on one another usually split apart faith and love, and whenever that happens in a church, the people have chosen to blind themselves to the great "what is" revealed in Jesus Christ.

In like manner, the concern for justice in the world is itself to be judged by the preeminence of love. True justice is built upon the foundation of authentic love. Love, however, is mostly a sentimental pretense if it ignores or violates the requirements of justice. Yet justice must always be subject to the suffering love of God for humanity. Thus, "The whole of theology should be irradiated by the principle 'God is love' understood as Jesus understood it," declared Pfister.[5] The ends never justify the means, even when the end has to do with issues of justice. The reason is that inauthentic or unjust means can never truly produce just ends. The result will only be a shadow of the desired end. To produce true justice one must act justly or deal with others in full integrity.

The love of God inspires hatred of evil in *all* its forms, but the battle against evil must never be fought with an evil spirit or with methods that violate the rights and the dignity or worth of other persons. Only by choosing to be blind to the "what is" of God in Christ can the people of God give in to an evil spirit in their fight against evil in the world. How pitiful it is to see a church or a whole denomination wandering around blind in both eyes, raging against evil while possessed of an evil spirit, or promoting programs of social justice with the power tactics of unchristian politics, while totally lacking the dynamic of suffering love that was the heart and soul of the transforming power of Jesus and the early church in challenging the world.

Cautions against the use of loveless power tactics in church politics should not be taken to mean that Christians should withdraw from political action in relation to the domain of the state. The marriage of justice and love is the Christian's best witness to the lordship of Christ in matters of public policy and in the forging of laws for a country. The state is meant to be subject to the claims of love and authenticity as surely as is the church. While every organization lives and works through patterns of power, the powers of the state, as of the church, may be used to serve either the blind ambition and self-interest of those who wield the power or may be harnessed to reflect com-

passion of people for one another. Just as the spirit lives in and
through the body, so the Spirit of God lives and works in and
through the body of society. That body is made up of many
members, including both church and state. Certainly in respect to the church particularly, but also to society as a whole,
the body functions at its best when its eyes are wide open to the
"what is" of the needs of people. To have open eyes means to
become sensitive to the transforming power of the love of God.
In such a pattern the body then serves the deepest longings
which God has placed within human hearts.

Fear and Seeing Reality as a Christian

As Christians, our calling is to face reality squarely. Transforming love is the only adequate means for dealing effectively
with a fear-oriented society and with a fearful church. Following the crucifixion, as the disciples gathered together behind
locked doors fearful that those who put Jesus to death would
soon discover their hiding place, John tells us that Jesus came to
them and stood in their midst. Looking deeply into their fearful eyes He spoke to them the words of shalom—peace (John
20:19).

There is no doubt that John wanted his readers to understand that in this act the disciples were experiencing a vision of
God in Christ. As we have said earlier, when people confront
the living God their reaction is understandably fear. The hope
in such a context is that humans will hear the words of the
messenger, "Fear not" or "Peace be with you." In this post-
resurrection appearance John did not concentrate on the disciples' fear of meeting God or His representative. They were already rendered powerless by their fear of the world. Instead,
he wrote only about the Lord's words of peace and the disciples' reaction of joy (vv. 19-20). But he added some additional
elements which provide insight into how you as a Christian are
to live in a world marked by fear.

The peace of Christ is set clearly within the context of the Lord's sending commission (v. 21). Christ knew that they feared the world and He gave to them His peace for their task. But, in addition, He also provided for them the promised Presence of the Holy Spirit in their lives (v. 22). Jesus was thus sending them back into a world which they feared, but he did not send them without a resource. That resource was none other than the accepting Presence of God in their inner selves, a Presence that would give them a sense of power and meaning in the midst of a fear-driven, manipulative, hurtful world. This Presence would enable them to live with pain, suffering, and hate and witness to the world and the church itself that greater is *He* that is *in you* than is in the world (1 John 4:4)!

This message of peace in the midst of turmoil, of love in the midst of fear, of hope in the midst of meaninglessness is the message of Christ Jesus our Lord. The Bible calls us to fear God and as a result to fear nothing else. To fear God is to sense His presence and to hear His commission to return with faith and hope and love to a world that is filled with distorted and meaningless fears. The final words in Matthew's Gospel testify powerfully to the same message. The departing Jesus summoned His disciples to return to the world and, in turn, disciple all nations, knowing that all power in the universe and in heaven itself is given to Jesus and is behind the work of Christians. But that power is not just outside of you because Jesus promised "Behold, I am present with you at all times until the very end of time itself" (Matt. 28:18-20).*

Go, therefore, Christian and fear not the world because you have come to terms with (you "fear") the greatest power in all of creation. That power is perfect Love that casts out fear.

Notes

Chapter 1
1. Earl A. Loomis, Jr., *The Self in Pilgrimage* (New York: Harper and Row, 1960), p. 1.

2. Elie Wiesel, *Night* (New York: Hill & Wang Publishers, 1960), p. 65.
Chapter 2
1. A story by Alan Jones in a lecture, May, 1987.
2. Gerald Borchert, *Assurance and Warning* (Nashville: Broadman Press, 1987), p. 212.
Chapter 3
1. Bernard Spilka, Ralph W. Hood, Jr., and Richard L. Gorsuch, *The Psychology of Religion: An Empirical Approach* (Englewood Cliffs: Prentice-Hall, Inc., 1985), pp. 19,27-28.
2. Ibid., pp. 270-274.
3. M. Scott Peck, *People of the Lie: The Hope for Healing Human Evil* (New York: Simon and Schuster, 1983), p. 76.
Chapter 4
1. Ana Maria Rizzuto, M.D. *The Birth of the Living God: A Psychoanalytic Study* (Chicago: The University of Chicago Press, 1979), pp. 93-108.
Chapter 5
1. For amplification of this theme see Edward E. Thornton, "Intimacy in Christian Life," *Review and Expositor*. Vol. LXXIV, No. 1 (Winter, 1977), pp. 43-59.
2. Borchert, pp. 128-129.
3. Dante, *Paradise* I. 1-3.
4. Adapted from Benjamin Hoff, *The Tao of Pooh* (New York: Penguin Books, 1982), pp. 134-137.
Chapter 6
1. The exercise is an adaptation of the Life Tapestry outline developed by the Center for Faith Development, Emory University, Atlanta, Georgia.
2. I. Shah, *Thinkers of the East* (London: Jonathan Capte, 1971), p. 176.
Chapter 7
1. Partial amplification of the four-stage process is drawn from Roberto Assagioli, *Psychosynthesis* (New York: Viking Press, 1965); and Bonnie Lee Hood, *Spiritual Emergencies* (Ed.D. Dissertation, The University of Massachusetts, May, 1986).
2. The criteria for discerning a spiritual surrender are drawn from Gerald G. May, M.D., *Will and Spirit: A Contemplative Psychology* (New York: Harper & Row, 1984), pp. 299-303.
3. *Meditations with T. M. Mechtild of Magdeburg,* versions by Sue Woodruff (Sante Fe: Bear & Company, 1982), p. 89.
Chapter 8
1. Pierre Teilhard de Chardin, *The Phenomenon of Man* (New York: Harper & Row), p. 169.
2. Charles Francis Whiston, *Teach Us to Pray*, with an Introduction by Nels F. S. Ferre (Boston: Pilgrim Press, 1948), pp. 115-134. Cited in Ronald V. Wells, *Spiritual Disciplines for Everyday Living* (Schenectady, N.Y.: Character Research Press, n.d.), pp. 51-53.
3. Ibid.
Chapter 9
1. George Bird Grinnell, *Pawnee Hero Stories and Folk-Tales* (Lincoln, Neb.: University of Nebraska Press, 1961), pp. 87-97.
2. Compare Edward E. Thornton, *Theology and Pastoral Counseling* (Englewood Cliffs, N.J.: Prentice-Hall, 1964), pp. 116-118.
Chapter 10
1. *Paradise* XXXIII, 136-145.
2. Thomas R. Kelly, *A Testament of Devotion* (San Francisco: Harper & Row, 1941).
3. Kelly, *The Eternal Promise*, p. 111.
4. Oscar Pfister, *Christianity and Fear* (London: George Allen & Unwin Ltd., 1948), p. 531.
5. Ibid., p. 544.